Why Human Nature Matters

WHY PHILOSOPHY MATTERS

Series editor: Professor Constantine Sandis,
University of Hertfordshire, UK

Why Philosophy Matters focuses on why a particular philosopher, school of thought, or area of philosophical study really matters. Each book will offer a brief overview of the subject before exploring its reception both within and outside the academy and our authors will also defend different provocative outlooks on where the value of philosophy lies (or doesn't, as the case may be). Why Philosophy Matters is accompanied by an ongoing series of free events (talks, debates, workshops) in Bloomsbury. Podcasts of these events will be freely available on the series page.

Books in this series
Why Iris Murdoch Matters, Gary Browning
Why Medieval Philosophy Matters, Stephen Boulter
Why Solipsism Matters, Sami Pihlström
Why Climate Breakdown Matters, Rupert Read
Why Cicero Matters, Vittorio Bufacchi
Why Delusions Matter, Lisa Bortolotti
Why Collingwood Matters, Giuseppina D'Oro

Also available from Bloomsbury
The Ahuman Manifesto, Patricia MacCormack
Philosophical Posthumanism, Francesca Ferrando

Why Human Nature Matters

Between Biology and Politics

Matteo Mameli

BLOOMSBURY ACADEMIC
LONDON • NEW YORK • OXFORD • NEW DELHI • SYDNEY

BLOOMSBURY ACADEMIC
Bloomsbury Publishing Plc
50 Bedford Square, London, WC1B 3DP, UK
1385 Broadway, New York, NY 10018, USA
29 Earlsfort Terrace, Dublin 2, Ireland

BLOOMSBURY, BLOOMSBURY ACADEMIC and the Diana logo
are trademarks of Bloomsbury Publishing Plc

First published in Great Britain 2024

For legal purposes the Acknowledgments on p. vii constitute
an extension of this copyright page.

Cover image: A monograph on the sub-class Cirripedia (barnacles) illustrated by
Charles Darwin. (Credit: Biodiversity Heritage Library / Public Domain)

A catalogue record for this book is available from the British Library.

A catalog record for this book is available from the Library of Congress.

ISBN: HB: 978-1-3501-8974-4
PB: 978-1-3501-8975-1
ePDF: 978-1-3501-8976-8
eBook: 978-1-3501-8977-5

Series: Why Philosophy Matters

Typeset by Integra Software Services Pvt. Ltd.
Printed and bound in Great Britain

Contents

Part Two

Acknowledgments

I am very grateful to Lorenzo Del Savio for his suggestions and for all the conversations we have had on the themes of this book. I would like to thank all those who offered comments or with whom I discussed some of the thoughts that have found their way into this work, including: Kim Sterelny, Giovanni Boniolo, David Papineau, Giorgio Cesarale, Giulia Cavaliere, Federico Boem, Tommaso Bruni, and Tom Pink; and I would like to remember the late Pat Bateson and Umberto Eco. I am grateful to the series editor, Constantine Sandis, and everybody at Bloomsbury, especially Liza Thomson, Lucy Russell, and Katrina Calsado. Thanks also go to my students and colleagues in the Department of Philosophy at King's College London, for the constant intellectual stimulation they provide. I could not have written this book without the unwavering support of my family.

Introduction

"Human nature matters because it constrains our lives and social interactions"; "human nature matters because it contains many unexpressed potentialities"; "human nature is immutable"; "human nature is what we make of it"; "human nature does not exist." Which of these claims are true? What is the best way to think about these issues?

We can use as a starting point some remarks made by the Italian Marxist Antonio Labriola:

> Men, living socially, do not cease to live in nature. They are not, of course, bound to nature as animals are, because they live on an artificial terrain. [...] But nature is always the immediate subsoil of the artificial terrain, and it is the ambit that fences us all. Technology has interposed between us social animals, and nature, the modifiers, the deviators, the repellers of the natural influxes; but it has not for all that destroyed their efficacy, and we continually feel such efficacy.[1]

Labriola believes that the "natural influxes" comprise both external and internal conditions, both those factors that come from outside and those that come from within our own human bodies.

At the end of the nineteenth century, Labriola coins the phrase *philosophy of praxis* to describe what he considers the "kernel" of Karl Marx and Friedrich Engels's philosophical outlook.[2] Some decades later, Antonio Gramsci, in his prison notebooks, borrows Labriola's phrase to refer to his own understanding and original elaboration of Marx's philosophical views.[3] Gramsci's views on human praxis constitute one of the pinnacles of politico-philosophical reflection in the twentieth century. Nevertheless, according to Sebastiano Timpanaro, Gramsci's philosophy of praxis involves a problematic "attenuation of materialism" compared to what can be found in Labriola.[4] This is despite the fact that Labriola's emphasis on the transformative potential of actions and thoughts is itself a reaction to the positivistic, fatalistic, and pseudo-evolutionistic varieties of Marxist materialism that had become influential at the end of the nineteenth century.[5]

In Gramsci, says Timpanaro, there is a "lack of materialism" because, in his attempt to elaborate an original philosophy for Marxism, Gramsci "concedes too much to idealism." According to Timpanaro, Gramsci's "attenuation of materialism" is "that characteristic most closely linked to the cultural contingencies of the milieu in which he lived."[6] Timpanaro explains:

> There has been a profoundly anti-materialist Gramsci, son of an epoch [...] in which materialism was equated with coarseness, good sense inherited from Catholicism ("if there is a reality outside and independent of us, it means God created it"), and in which it seemed possible to defeat politically right-wing idealism only by elaborating an activistic idealism that emphasized the moment of praxis and insisted, rather than on nature as an object of knowledge "posited" by the subject, on nature as an object of man-made transformation.[7]

Gramsci uses the phrase "vulgar materialism" to criticize "fatalistic," "mechanical," "mechanistic," "deterministic," "metaphysical" versions of materialism.[8] On his view, these forms of materialism inevitably lead to political "passivity" and are a "religion of the subalterns."[9] Gramsci considers materialism to be closer to religious accounts of reality than is idealism. He writes:

> According to the Bible [...] not only was the world created before Adam, but God created it for him. Religion, then, cannot distance itself from the view that "reality" exists independently of the thinking individual.[10]

The Gramscian philosophy of praxis appears incompatible with what Timpanaro refers to as "rigorous materialism." Rigorous materialism acknowledges not only the significance of human transformative powers but also the ways in which certain aspects of our bodies and the environments we inhabit can frustrate our projects and aspirations. Rigorous materialism, moreover, appeals to the so-called "natural sciences" to come to grips with these aspects of reality.[11] But all this does not mean that the term "praxis" should be abandoned. This term, with its multifaceted history, is sufficiently flexible and can be appropriated by those seeking to pursue a rigorously materialist strategy. It can be utilized to draw attention not only to the different ways in which humans transform the world but also to the concrete materiality of these processes. Human praxis is embodied, and it is embedded within broad ecological, planetary, and cosmic contexts. A thoroughly materialist philosophy of praxis is both (conceptually) possible and (philosophically and politically) desirable.[12]

One way to develop this idea is to explore how Labriola's metaphor can help build a bridge between a rigorously materialist philosophy of human praxis and the theory of *niche construction*. As Odling-Smee, Laland, and Feldman put it:

> All living creatures, through their metabolism, their activities, and their choices, partly create and partly destroy their own niches, on scales ranging from the extremely local to the global. Organisms choose habitats and resources, construct aspects of their environments such as nests, holes, burrows, webs, pupal cases, and a chemical milieu, and frequently choose, protect, and provision nursery environments for their offspring. [...] All organisms must interact with their environments to stay alive, and [...] when they do, it is not just organisms that are likely to be affected by the consequences of these interactions, but also environments. [...] Organisms actively contribute toward both the "construction" and "destruction" of their own and each other's niches.[13]

The accumulated effects of the activities (and "choices") of the organisms of one species can have a multigenerational impact on that same species or on other species. Organisms inherit genetic material from their parents, but they also inherit the outcomes of the choices and activities of their conspecifics and non-conspecifics. Such inherited outcomes frequently affect ontogenetic processes and the chances of surviving and reproducing. In other words, multigenerational niche construction transforms both the developmental environments of organisms and the evolutionary selection pressures acting upon them. Niche construction modifies the distribution of developmental factors, as well as the intensity and direction of selection processes. Childhood vaccines, for example, affect the development of human immune systems and change the selection pressures acting on humans (and viruses). Vaccines are part of the niche that humans have built via the accumulated activities of many individuals (and institutions, which are themselves the result of the accumulated activities of individuals).

Important ideas concerning niche construction can be found in Charles Darwin's books and, in particular, in his final one, *The*

Formation of Vegetable Mould through the Action of Worms. Darwin argues that the soil-digesting activities of earthworms create "the layer of vegetable mould, which covers the whole surface of the land in every moderately humid country."[14] This layer is hugely important for plant and animal life, and thereby for the whole ecosystem. Earthworms partially construct their own niche and the niche of many other living beings:

> I was thus led to conclude that all the vegetable mould over the whole country has passed many times through, and will again pass many times through, the intestinal canals of worms. Hence the term "animal mould" would be in some respects more appropriate than that commonly used of "vegetable mould." [...] When we behold a wide, turf-covered expanse, we should remember that its smoothness, on which so much of its beauty depends, is mainly due to all the inequalities having been slowly levelled by worms. It is a marvellous reflection that the whole of the superficial mould over any such expanse has passed, and will again pass, every few years through the bodies of worms. The plough is one of the most ancient and most valuable of man's inventions; but long before he existed the land was in fact regularly ploughed, and still continues to be thus ploughed by earth-worms. It may be doubted whether there are many other animals which have played so important a part in the history of the world, as have these lowly organised creatures.[15]

Darwin refers to the "small agencies [of earthworms] and their accumulated effects."[16] Without intending to intellectualize earthworms, we can call this phenomenon *earthworm praxis*. In relation to changes in their conditions of life, both internal and external, corporeal and extracorporeal, organisms are both subjects and objects, agents and patients, sources as well as recipients of change.[17] This is true of all living praxis, not just human praxis.

Even though he considers it an exclusively human phenomenon, Labriola conceives of human praxis in niche-constructionist terms:

> Man *develops*—that is, *produces*—himself not as a being generically provided with certain attributes, which repeat or develop themselves according to a rational rhythm; he develops and produces himself as at once cause and effect, as author and consequence of certain definite conditions.[18]

Like the majority of his contemporaries, Labriola misses the niche-constructionist ideas that can be found in Darwin's work. The Italian thinker sees the Darwinian "transmutation of species" as something externally determined. He explains why, in his view, praxis is exclusively human:

> Man is distinctively the experimental animal; that is why he has a history, or rather that is why he makes his own history.[19]

Labriola fails to acknowledge that earthworms also have a history—a history that they have partially made and that has affected the history of many other beings on Planet Earth. Nevertheless, there is no denying that human praxis is, in some respects, distinctive. It is through characteristics not found in other species—such as speech, writing, culture, science, technology, rationality—that we have expanded our habitat range and invaded the whole globe, changed the living conditions of our own and many other species, and brought about modifications in various geological and climatic processes on a planetary scale. Human niche construction has profoundly transformed both humans and the rest of nature, with the pace of transformation continually accelerating. Finding the right way to grasp the similarities and differences between human niche construction and the niche-constructing processes of other species is of utmost importance.

In the current epoch of genetic and molecular engineering, anthropogenic climate change, and ecological collapse, the human planetary footprint is becoming every day more evident. Will we destroy our conditions of life and cause our own extinction? Will we bio-engineer our bodies and those of other living organisms? Will we geo-engineer Planet Earth? Will we be able to remove the barriers that separate us and other terrestrial beings from better modes of life? Will we revolutionize our praxis? If so, in what ways?

*

The elaboration, modification, and spread of ideas about human nature is a part of human praxis that shapes other parts of human praxis and that, by doing so, conditions the ways we live, including the ways we organize and reorganize our social systems and our interactions with the rest of nature. Symbols can be causally powerful, including those symbols with which we humans think about ourselves as members of a species. Non-human organisms can condition their modes of life through their praxis, including their communicative behaviors, but they have not (until now) been able to condition their modes of life through a conception of the world containing ideas about their own species nature.[20]

Human ideas about human nature can have a *conservative* or a *transformative* impact on human modes of life. It is useful to invoke Labriola again. After having told us that the natural "subsoil" should not be ignored, he tells us something about how he conceives of this "subsoil":

> As we are born naturally male and female, as we die almost always in spite of ourselves, and as we are dominated by the instinct of generation, so we also bear in our temperament certain specific conditions, which education in the broad sense of the word [...] can modify, within certain limits, but can never destroy. These

> conditions of temperament, repeated in many individuals and transmitted throughout the centuries, constitute what is called ethnic character.[21]

There are portions of the "subsoil" that cannot be entirely and properly digested by human earthworms. Among these portions, there are, says Labriola, the male/female divide, the desire not to die, the "instinct of reproduction," and what he calls "ethnic character." Nowadays, we know that suicidal tendencies are culturally and environmentally plastic, and so are the desire to have (or not to have) sex and the desire to have (or not to have) biologically related children, which are distinct desires. We also know that many important elements of the human male/female divide, as well as those population differences that Labriola describes in terms of "ethnic character," are profoundly shaped by social factors and are in some respects extremely malleable.

The view that there are hard-to-modify ethnic "temperaments," possibly resulting from the biological inheritance of acquired traits, was influential in Labriola's time. This view contributed to those conflicts that reached some of their most tragic peaks during the two world wars of the first half of the twentieth century. Labriola expressed support for some of the colonialist policies of the Italian government. According to Timpanaro, Labriola's belief in the "scientific validity" of the idea of unplastic ethnic temperaments "contributed to provoking those colonialist aberrations which remain the most disconcerting and negative aspect of Labriola's thought and action."[22]

The belief in an unplastic human nature is often assumed to lead to a pro-status-quo stance, but this assumption is not warranted. Consider the view that there are fixed natural differences between men and women and that, due to this, any attempt to eliminate existing gender inequalities in the distribution of social goods is bound to fail and cause social problems. Those who hold this view might recommend maintaining the status quo; alternatively, they might argue that there is already too much gender parity and that we should have less of it. They could propose emulating some past gender-unequal society (which would be a *reactionary* proposal) or they could advocate some entirely novel gender-unequal arrangements, arguing that such arrangements would more closely fit the natural differences between the sexes. Similarly, those who believe in fixed population differences in "temperament" or intelligence (differences that "education in the broad sense of the world […] can never destroy") might dislike the status quo. They might argue that populations with a superior "ethnic character" ought to subjugate inferior populations, with the aim of building better societies. Pro-colonization views, even when rooted in a belief in fixed natural differences, are not always (or even typically) in favor of the status quo.

Invoking human nature does not necessarily mean opposing social change. But if you believe that invoking human nature leads to politically undesirable forms of praxis, you might want to argue that human nature does not exist and that we should abandon the language of human nature. This is *political eliminativism* about human nature. Eliminativism about human nature can also stem from nonpolitical motivations. A nonpolitical eliminativist believes that, regardless of their political implications, standard ways of thinking about human nature are misleading, and that it is not desirable to seek an alternative.

Disentangling political and nonpolitical (conceptual, factual, etc.) reasons for eliminativism about human nature is often difficult. Both forms of eliminativism are frequently attributed to Marx, but this attribution is misplaced. Marx is certainly critical of standard ways of thinking about human nature, but he does not claim that it does not exist. Instead, he writes:

> All history is nothing but a continuous transformation of human nature.[23]

> By [...] acting on the external world and changing it, he [man] at the same time changes his own nature.[24]

Gramsci endorses this Marxian view in his prison notebooks, where he writes:

> The basic innovation introduced by Marx into the science of politics and of history [...] is the demonstration that a fixed and immutable "human nature" does not exist.[25]

Both Marx and Gramsci claim that standard ways of thinking about human nature, which portray it as fixed and immutable, should be rejected. Both suggest that we should replace these standard ways of thinking not with eliminativist attitudes, but rather with ways of thinking that characterize human nature as mutable. Moreover, both philosophers argue that the mutability of human nature is of a distinctive kind: humans can transform their nature in ways that are not accessible to other organisms. Marx, who is the source of Labriola's thoughts on human distinctiveness, emphasizes the transformative role of human "labour":

> Labour is, in the first place, a process in which both man and Nature participate, and in which man of his own accord starts, regulates, and controls the material reactions between himself and Nature. He opposes himself to Nature as one of her own forces, setting in motion arms and legs, head and hands, the natural forces of his body, in order to appropriate Nature's productions in a form adapted to his own wants. By thus acting on the external world and changing it, he at the same time changes his own nature.[26]

Gramsci also emphasizes human transformative powers, but he does so in ways that "attenuate" the materialist elements found in Marx:

> As for this expression "historical materialism", greater stress is placed on the second word, whereas it should be placed on the first: Marx is fundamentally a "historicist".[27]

> It has been forgotten that in the case of a very common expression ["historical materialism"] one should put the accent on the first term—"historical"—and not on the second, which is of metaphysical origin. The philosophy of praxis is absolute "historicism," the absolute secularisation and earthliness of thought, an absolute humanism of history. It is along this line that one must trace the thread of the new conception of the world.[28]

According to Gramsci, we should not refer to "matter as such" in our philosophical accounts. We should not speak of matter as it is dealt with in the "natural sciences." We should instead only refer to matter as "socially and historically organized."[29] Arguably, despite his reference to "earthliness," Gramsci's philosophy of praxis is not "earthly" enough.[30]

A view that draws attention to the ways in which human nature can mutate is better than an eliminativist approach. However, for a view of human nature as mutable through praxis to work, one needs to acknowledge not just the transformative impact of human praxis but also its concrete materiality. We need to avoid seeing human nature as something rigid and unchangeable; at the same time, we need to reject any "attenuation of materialism."

*

In Part One of this book, I explore various classic perspectives on human nature, featuring ideas from Aristotle, Augustine, Hobbes, Rousseau, Marx, Engels, and others. The discussion shows how debates about human nature are often debates concerning the ways humans can or cannot cooperate and the ways our nature enables or constrains the social production (and reproduction) of valuable human goods and relations. Ideas about human nature often have a profound influence on how we continuously recreate and govern our modes of life.

In Part Two, I make an intervention in contemporary discussions on the concept (or notion, or conception) of human nature. This part of the book criticizes various proposals concerning how we should think about human nature in abstract terms, and it makes an alternative proposal—one that focuses on plasticity, diversity, and transformative processes. In today's context, ideas about human nature cannot be isolated from evolutionary biology and the sciences of human biocultural differences, as long as these sciences are understood in fully niche-constructionist terms. At the same time, a good way of thinking about human nature needs to consider the role played by ideas about human nature in social conflict and in structuring our modes of life.

In the Conclusions, I revisit Timpanaro's critique of Gramsci's attenuated materialism and the general issues concerning human nature, human modes of life, and the embeddedness of human praxis.

Part One

1

Cooperation

Social Beings

Descriptions of human modes of life, and of which modes of life might be accessible to us, have an impact on human praxis. Marx writes:

> Man is a *zôon politikon* in the most literal sense: he is not only a social animal, but an animal that can isolate itself only within society. Production by an isolated individual outside society—something rare, which might occur when a civilised person already dynamically in possession of the social forces is accidentally cast into the wilderness—is just as preposterous as the development of language without individuals who live together and speak to one another.[1]

Individualistic modes of life, according to Marx, are highly social modes of life. Even a Robinson Crusoe on a desert island has a social mode of life insofar as he possesses language and other cognitive tools created and developed socially. Recognizing this has implications for how we collectively govern our lives. There is no pre-social mode of life in humans. In this passage, Marx is criticizing the "Robinsonades" of Adam Smith and David Ricardo, and their claims about how market exchanges can emerge spontaneously as a result of selfish pre-social motives.[2]

Another critical target of Marx's views is Thomas Hobbes. Hobbes writes in *Leviathan* that in "the naturall condition" humans live "without a common Power to keep them all in awe" and thus:

> They are in that condition which is called Warre; and such a warre, as is of every man, against every man.[3]

Hobbes explains:

> In such condition, there is no place for Industry; because the fruit thereof is uncertain: and consequently no Culture of the Earth; no

> Navigation, nor use of the commodities that may be imported by Sea; no commodious Building; no Instruments of moving, and removing such things as require much force; no Knowledge of the face of the Earth; no account of Time; no Arts; no Letters; no Society; and which is worst of all, continuall feare, and danger of violent death; And the life of man, solitary, poore, nasty, brutish, and short.[4]

Many important human goods are absent in the state of nature. In *De Cive*, Hobbes writes:

> Men's natural Disposition is such that if they are not restrained by fear of a common power, they will distrust and fear each other [...] The majority of previous writers on public Affairs either assume or seek to prove or simply assert that Man is an animal born fit for Society [*aptum natum ad Societatem*]—in the Greek phrase, *zôon politikon*. [...] This Axiom, though very widely accepted, is nevertheless false; the error proceeds from a superficial view of human nature.[5]

The fear of one another is a fear of death—of being killed by others—and it is equivalent to being constantly in a state of war against others. This constant fear exists not because humans are fundamentally evil or cruel, but rather, according to Hobbes, because humans are fundamentally equal, both in terms of physical strength and in terms of mental capabilities:

> Nature hath made men so equall, in the faculties of body, and mind; as that though there bee found one man sometimes manifestly stronger in body, or of quicker mind then another; yet when all is reckoned together, the difference between man, and man, is not so considerable, as that one man can thereupon claim to himselfe any benefit, to which another may not pretend, as well as he. For as to the strength of body, the weakest has strength enough to kill the strongest, either by secret machination, or by confederacy with

> others, that are in the same danger with himselfe. And as to the faculties of the mind, [...] I find yet a greater equality amongst men, than that of strength. [...] From this equality of ability, ariseth equality of hope in the attaining of our Ends. And therefore if any two men desire the same thing, which nevertheless they cannot both enjoy, they become enemies; and in the way to their End (which is principally their owne conservation, and sometimes their delectation only,) endeavour to destroy or subdue one an other.[6]

We often desire for ourselves what others desire for themselves. The fact that differences in strength and intelligence are generally small means, on this view, that any human can potentially harm or even kill any other human to obtain what they desire, and to protect themselves from other people's desires. Every human has reasons to accumulate as much power as possible.

The war of all against all is a possible mode of life. It is, according to Hobbes, the inevitable mode of human life in the absence of a sovereign power. Stable forms of cooperation only emerge when the disjointed members of the multitude, motivated by the desire to avoid the "perpetual diffidence" and the "continuall feare" of death, agree to subject themselves to a sovereign power and relinquish their freedom. Through a "covenant," the right to govern oneself is transferred to a sovereign power, which can be either "one man" or an "assembly." If it is an assembly, it can include either all the members of the multitude or just some.[7] Hobbes's preference is for the "one man" solution: the unlimited and undivided sovereign power of a single individual is the best way "to produce the Peace, and Security, of the people."[8]

The "covenant" creates "that great Leviathan called a Common-wealth, or STATE, (in latine *Civitas*) which is but an Artificiall Man."[9] In the lower part of the frontispiece of the first edition of *De Cive* (Figure 1), *Libertas* is represented by an Indigenous American

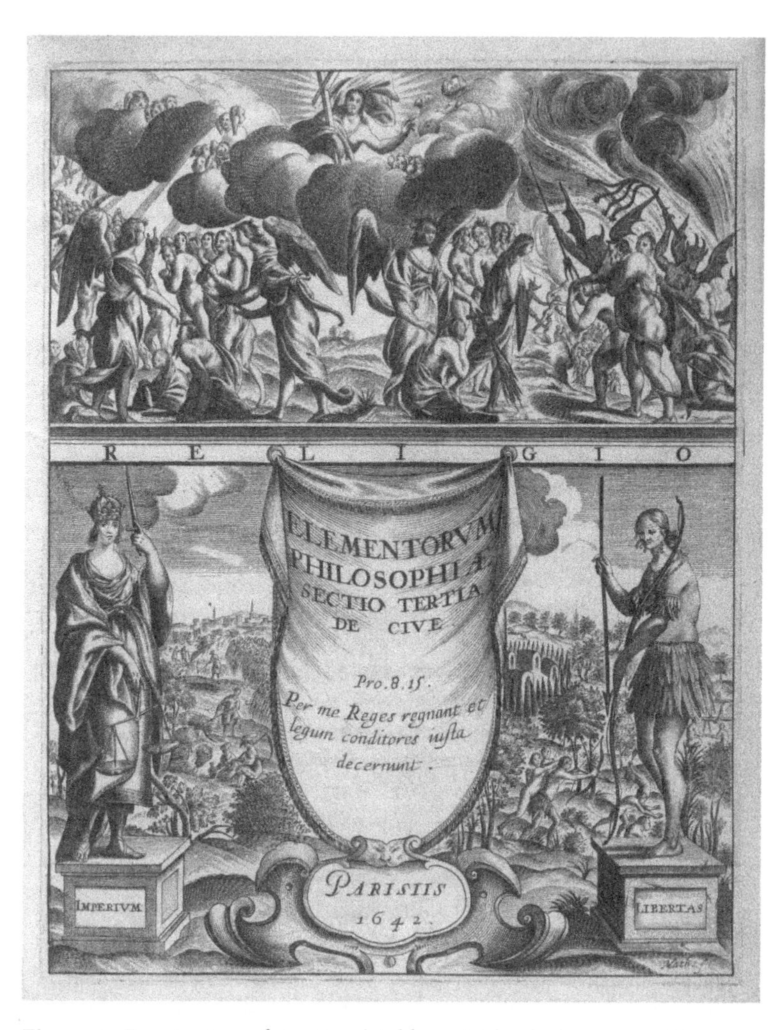

Figure 1 *Frontispiece of De Cive (Hobbes 1642). The lower part illustrates the contrast between IMPERIUM and LIBERTAS. The upper part represents the Last Judgment, suggesting that all modes of human life need to be understood and evaluated in relation to that event. For a discussion, see Skinner 2009; Moloney 2011. Image courtesy of EC65 H6525 642e, Houghton Library, Harvard University.*

woman, with a wrinkled face and an anxious (or possibly threatening) expression. She is wearing a short, feathered skirt and armlets, and holding a bow and a spear. The landscape behind her depicts naked humans hunting other naked humans with bows and arrows, and naked humans dismembering other naked humans. In contrast, *Imperium* is represented by a peaceful-looking, smooth-skinned woman. She has a crown, a sword, and a scale—symbols of justice and sovereignty. The landscape beside her features people working in fields, people resting, and, in the distance, the tall buildings of a town.

Hobbes claims that "the naturall condition" can be found in the Indigenous populations of America:

> For the savage people in many places of *America*, except the government of small Families, the concord whereof depends on natural lust, have no government at all, and live at this day in that brutish manner.[10]

Hobbes concedes that there are forms of association and cooperation in these "savage" populations—forms of association and cooperation that "men are born fit for." He explains:

> It is indeed true that perpetual solitude is hard for a man to bear by nature or as a man, i.e. as soon as he is born. For infants need the help of others to live, and adults to live well. I am not therefore denying that we seek each other's company at the prompting of nature. But civil Societies are not mere gatherings; they are Alliances [*Foedera*], which essentially require good faith and agreement for their making.[11]

Humans in their natural condition are not *entirely* non-social and not *entirely* devoid of cooperation; but, according to Hobbes, such a condition is characterized by forms of cooperation that are unstable and have limited productive potential. An artificial (non-natural) sovereign power—a single will that stands above the multiplicity of conflicting wills—can stabilize cooperation, including cooperation within families.[12] The level of stability afforded by a sovereign power generates the kind of productive potential that can be observed in "civil Society."

Hobbes and Marx agree that the production of important human goods and relations is a cooperative endeavor, but they disagree on what is required to make this endeavor possible and efficient. Marx does not endorse the idea that submission to an absolute and undivided sovereign power maximizes the potentialities of human social production. From a Marxian perspective, there is no reason to think that the state constitutes a significant discontinuity in relation to the stability of human cooperation. Furthermore, according to Marx, there are reasons to believe that humans can achieve large-scale forms of stable cooperation that dispense with the state, or at least with some of its worst features. According to Marx, all the forms of cooperation that humans have acquired to this day are, to some extent, impoverished, since they fall short of the form of cooperation in which "the free development of each is the condition for the free development of all."[13]

Within a Marxian framework, insofar as it makes sense to say that humans are "born fit for" some forms of cooperation, all the forms of cooperation that humans have been able to access until now are such that humans are born fit for them. However, in this sense, humans can also be said to be born fit for forms of cooperation that they have not yet achieved and that, if achieved, would unleash greater productive potentials. According to Marx, current forms of cooperation are inferior forms of cooperation; they are wasteful in that they do not allow our bodies and minds to freely and frictionlessly produce (and benefit from) all the great human goods that we could potentially produce (and benefit from).[14]

Political Animals

One reason to contrast Marx with Hobbes is that both refer to the Aristotelian thesis according to which humans are by nature political animals (*phusei politikon zôon*).[15] Hobbes rejects the Aristotelian thesis, whereas Marx presents himself as endorsing it. The meaning and the implications of the Aristotelian thesis are highly disputed.[16] Nevertheless, it is useful to examine its claims.

Aristotle employs the phrase *phusei politikon zôon* with reference to humans, but also with reference to non-human living beings. He asserts that bees, wasps, ants, and also cranes are political.[17] To qualify as political by nature, a group of conspecifics must meet various conditions: the animals must interact with each other to achieve a common goal (they must have a common work [*koinon ergon*]); the cooperative interactions must involve a division of labor (the common work must involve different roles); and the animals must possess cognitive and emotional capacities that facilitate, and find their best expression in, these cooperative interactions and the achievement of the common goal.[18] Bees, wasps, ants, and cranes meet these conditions, according to the Stagirite. These living beings lack a *polis*, but they have a common work and a common goal, they have a division of labor, and they have capacities that find their best expression in such common work. Political animals differ from other kinds of gregarious animals, such as herding animals, which live together and form groups but do not have a common work.[19]

Even though some non-human animals can be said to be political, humans are, says Aristotle, "political in a greater measure." Humans are more intensely (and more appropriately termed) political because they have "speech" (*logos*), as opposed to the other animals, which only have "voice." We have linguistic and reasoning skills that allow us to make distinctions between good and bad, and between just and unjust.[20] As a result of this, we have a distinctive kind of common work; this is what language and reason are for, since "nature [...] does nothing without a purpose." The goal of the human common work is a form of collective self-sufficiency aimed not just at "life" (mere survival) but at "good life."[21] It is the form of cooperation that characterizes the *polis* that can give rise to this.

The *polis* is the "most supreme" (most authoritative, highest-ranking) form of human association.[22] It comprises within itself other forms of cooperation, such as households, clans, and villages. Those other forms of cooperation are small scale and are unable to reliably result in the relevant kind of self-sufficiency, but they are "for the sake of" the *polis*. Nature, according to Aristotle, is organized teleologically, which in relation to human associations means that there is a tendency for human cooperation to reach the special kind of self-sufficiency that can only be obtained within and through the *polis*. The *polis* is a "natural growth" and it is the mature (fully actualized) form of a natural entity whose immature developmental stages (and parts) are the household, the clan, and the village.[23] These incomplete kinds of cooperation are affected, and made possible, by the linguistic and reasoning capacities that are involved in *polis*-level cooperation. However, in these incomplete kinds of cooperation, such capacities do not find their full expression. This, in and of itself, makes it impossible for the good life to be achieved via these incomplete forms of cooperation.[24]

Within this global teleological framework, humans are said to have an "impulse" (*hormê*) to create and participate in the form of cooperation that constitutes the *polis*; that is, humans have an internal drive to create and participate in what Aristotle considers the highest-ranking form of human cooperation.[25] Humans who lack this internal drive are, therefore, "by nature and not merely by fortune citiless."

These individuals are not fully human, since they cannot fully develop and exercise those human capacities that non-human animals lack and that allow (some) humans to achieve the most complete way of being human. These capacities, when properly developed and exercised, make humans "the best of all animals"; humans become "the worst of all" when such capacities are not properly exercised in the common work that constitutes the *polis*.[26]

Within this framework, in order to fully grasp human nature, one needs to understand what humans are at their best, in the context of (what Aristotle takes to be) the best form of specifically human cooperation.

*

In reaction to the Aristotelian notion of a natural tendency toward forms of *polis*-like cooperation, Hobbes denies that "Man is an animal born fit for Society." According to Hobbes, humans might be "born fit" for unstable and small-scale forms of cooperation with an impoverished productive potential, such as those resulting from "natural lust." Nevertheless, humans are certainly not born fit for stable and prosperity-generating large-scale forms of cooperation, such as the *polis* or the *commonwealth*. In the context of this discussion, Hobbes makes some important anti-Aristotelian comments on ants and bees:

> Among the animals which Aristotle calls political he counts not only Man but many others too, including the Ant, the Bee, etc. For although they are devoid of reason, which would enable them to make agreements and submit to government [*regimen*], still by their consenting, i.e. by desiring and avoiding the same objects, they so direct their actions to a common end that their swarms are not disturbed by sedition. Yet their swarms are still not commonwealths [*civitates*], and so the animals themselves

> should not be called political; for their government is only an accord, or many wills with one object, not (as a commonwealth needs) one will.[27]

Hobbes agrees that some non-human animals cooperate productively in sophisticated and stable ways, and that they do so peacefully. However, Hobbes argues, this is not enough to classify these animals as truly political. The peaceful and stable cooperation within an ant or bee colony occurs because all the members of the collective just happen to want what is good for the colony. In contrast, a genuinely political collective contains numerous conflicting wills desiring incompatible things. In such a collective, peaceful and stable cooperation can only emerge when a single will rises above the disjointed multiplicity of separate wills. Humans can artificially create this single will through a covenant, which requires language and reason; ants and bees cannot do this, and at the same time they do not need to do this.

One might concede that the term "political" should not be applied to bees and ants; but, if being genuinely political makes peaceful and stable cooperation difficult to achieve, humans should not pride themselves on being genuinely political and should consider how to be peacefully cooperative in the ways that the bees and the ants are. Hobbes explains that humans (without God's help) cannot be peacefully and stably cooperative in the apolitical ways of insect colonies. In doing so, he clarifies the ways in which humans are genuinely political. Unlike bees and ants, humans engage in competition for status. Humans desire distinction and preeminence because, unlike bees and ants, and as a result of the way language augments their cognition, humans can think about the future and are concerned about their long-term security. The pursuit of distinction and preeminence serves as a means of self-protection. The lack of linguistic communication also means that bees and ants are unable to criticize their form of government, whereas humans often do this and argue that things could be better if social arrangements were changed. Hobbes notes that this can lead to useful social innovations, but it also gives rise to sedition and forms of social instability that are absent in insect colonies.[28]

For Aristotle, language and reason make humans more political than ants and bees. In contrast, for Hobbes, language and reason make humans uniquely political, but in a way that renders them unable to cooperate stably and productively without an artificial prosthesis (a sovereign power); the lack of language and reason makes ants and bees unable to be political, but blissfully so. Hobbesian humans are "citiless by nature" and, as a result, are not fully human from an Aristotelian viewpoint; they are marginal instances of humanity. Conversely, from a Hobbesian viewpoint, Aristotelian humans, or at least those who are considered fully human by Aristotle, appear entirely fictional.[29]

*

Marx disagrees with the claim that the *polis*, or the state, is the "most supreme" form of human cooperation. He believes that the dominant form of human cooperation of his own time—the coupling of the capitalist state and the world market—can in some ways be seen as an improvement over previous forms of large-scale cooperation. But he thinks that the best *possible* form of cooperation is still to come.[30] Neither the Greek *polis* (with its slaves) nor the capitalist system (with its wage laborers) is a form of cooperation where "the free development of each is the condition for the free development of all." Neither the Greek *polis* nor the capitalist system is an association where "the full and free development of every individual forms the ruling principle," where "the development of human energy" has become "an end in itself," or where "the springs of common wealth flow" without encountering barriers due to how we organize our modes of life.[31]

Would Marx agree with the claim that we have an "impulse" to bring about and participate in the "most supreme" form of cooperation, whatever that is? Given a rejection of teleological conceptions of nature, the Aristotelian argument for the existence of an internal drive of this sort is not available to Marx.[32] Nonetheless, Marx can be interpreted as endorsing one aspect of the Aristotelian view: in order to understand what we fundamentally are, we should, among other things, consider humans at their cooperative best—although for Marx we are still far from such a cooperative best, which remains an unexpressed potentiality. For different reasons and with different goals, both Marx and Aristotle reject the view that one can properly understand what we fundamentally are by focusing exclusively or primarily on humans at their antisocial worst.[33]

As for bees, Marx famously mentions them (alongside spiders) in *Capital*:

> A spider conducts operations that resemble those of a weaver, and a bee puts to shame many an architect in the construction of her cells. But what distinguishes the worst architect from the best of bees is this, that the architect raises his structure in imagination before he erects it in reality. At the end of every labour process, we get a result that already existed in the imagination of the labourer at its commencement. He not only effects a change of form in the material on which he works, but he also realises a purpose of his own that gives the law to his *modus operandi*, and to which he must subordinate his will.[34]

Marx is not discussing bee sociality here. From a materialist perspective that acknowledges important continuities between non-human and human animals, he is trying to pinpoint what he believes to be a significant discontinuity. The discontinuity is the human ability to imagine certain outcomes and create what one has imagined. If humans can do this and bees cannot, this is likely to affect the ways in which humans and bees can socially produce human and apian goods, respectively. On a view like this, human social production and bee social production are different as a result of this mental discontinuity.

In *The Part Played by Labour in the Transition from Ape to Man*, Engels writes:

> Animals [...] change the environment by their activities in the same way, even if not to the same extent, as man does, and these changes [...] in turn react upon and change those who made them. [...] But animals exert a lasting effect on their environment unintentionally and, as far as the animals themselves are concerned, accidentally. The further removed men are from animals, however, the more their effect on nature assumes the character of premeditated, planned action directed towards definite preconceived ends. [...] It goes without saying that it would not occur to us to dispute the ability of animals to act in a planned, premeditated fashion. [...] There is something of the planned action in the way insect-eating plants capture their prey, although they do it quite unconsciously. [...] But all the planned action of all animals has never succeeded in impressing the stamp of their will upon the earth. That was left for man.[35]

What is crucial here is the idea that human niche construction is, at least in some cases and in some respects, more powerfully transformative than the niche-constructing activities of non-human animals. Marx tries to explain this by referring to the imagination as a distinctive human trait. Engels tries to explain it by talking about the intentional production of changes in the world, and his oscillating remarks suggest that the difference is simply a matter of degree. There is "something of the planned action" in non-human animals; and, both in humans and in non-humans, behaviors often produce effects that are not in any way intended or desired by the agent.[36] However, our understanding of the world (including our understanding of human societies) and our understanding of how it is possible to change the world (including human societies) continuously evolve in cumulative ways. This is itself an outcome of human social production:

> With every day that passes we are acquiring a better understanding of these laws and getting to perceive both the more immediate and the more remote consequences of our interference with the traditional course of nature. [...] It required the labour of thousands of years for us to learn a little of how to calculate the more remote *natural* effects of our actions in the field of production, but it has been still more difficult in regard to the more remote *social* effects of these actions. [...] But in this sphere too, by long and often cruel experience and by collecting and analysing historical material, we are gradually learning to get a clear view of the indirect, more remote social effects of our production activity, and so are afforded an opportunity to control and regulate these effects as well.[37]

Bee social production does not result in a cumulatively evolving understanding of the impact of apian praxis on the world, a key difference between the bees and us.[38] It is due to this cumulatively evolving understanding that, when we think about what we fundamentally are, it makes sense to consider forms of cooperation that are still to come and that could be much better than what we currently have. Our understanding of praxis and its surrounding contexts helps us modulate our niche-constructing efforts in ways that are not available to the bees.[39]

The ways we transform our societies and the ways we transform the rest of nature are interconnected. According to the third volume of *Capital*: "that development of human energy which is an end in itself, the true realm of freedom," can be obtained only after the human "associated producers" start "rationally regulating their interchange with Nature, bringing it under their common control, instead of being ruled by it as by blind forces of Nature; and achieving this with the least expenditure of energy."[40] Nothing of the sort could ever happen to the apian associated producers (or to earthworms for that matter), unless they become able to constantly transform their understanding of their cooperative endeavors in the ways we do. In order to grasp what we fundamentally are, we need, among other things, to direct our attention to this cumulatively evolving understanding, and to the desirable forms of human cooperation that could, at least in principle, flow from it.

It is important to stress that the (performative) optimism of Marx and Engels may be partly or entirely unjustified. Our cumulatively evolving understanding could, after all, have disastrous consequences. The whole process could result in a "catastrophe piling wreckage upon wreckage" rather than in what is "most worthy and most favourable."[41] This issue remains open. Regardless, our reflections on what we fundamentally are need to pay proper attention to this process, and to its role within our cosmically embedded, world-digesting, and sediment-producing cooperative endeavors.

Superorganisms

The sociobiologist and myrmecologist Edward Osborne Wilson half-jokingly claims:

> Karl Marx was right, socialism works, it is just that he had the wrong species.[42]

Wilson's suggestion is that socialism and communism are not for humans but can be found in eusocial species. The vast majority of ant species, as well as many bee and wasp species, are eusocial. In paradigmatic eusocial colonies, only one or a small number of female individuals, the *queens*, reproduce. Males fertilize the queens; in many cases, males do not have other significant roles in the colony and die shortly after having fulfilled their fertilizing function. Most of the members of the colony are female *workers*. These are females that do not lay eggs. They are daughters of the queen and have specific jobs to do for the colony: looking for food and bringing it to the nest (or hive), building and repairing the nest, caring for the young, defending the nest from external attacks, and so on.[43]

In eusocial species, the division of labor between queens and sterile workers is rigid, in that there are mechanisms within the colony that inhibit egg-laying in the workers, including the removal of workers that attempt to lay eggs.[44] Eusocial colonies are sometimes said to be *superorganisms* because their functional organization is not too dissimilar from that found in complex multicellular organisms. In humans and many other animals there is a rigid separation between germline cells (which give rise to gametes and have a reproductive role) and somatic cells (which have a role in the building and functioning of the organism). Most cells—such as those making up the skin, the liver, the immune system, the brain—are somatic. In some cases, somatic cells start malfunctioning and end up dividing (reproducing) in uncontrolled ways. When this happens, the resulting cellular growth, which can be cancerous, can threaten bodily functions and kill the animal. This is similar in some respects to what happens when a eusocial sterile worker starts laying eggs and, by doing so, puts at risk the stability and survival of the colony. Somatic cells can be said to be the sterile workers of complex multicellular organisms. There are mechanisms with the function to eliminate such cells when they reproduce in rebellious ways and when they stop behaving as obedient sterile workers.[45]

Wilson sees eusocial colonies as instances of communist living because a eusocial colony is a social system where, in general, every sterile member works not for its own benefit but for the benefit of the colony and of its descendants. Every sterile member works for the survival of the colony and for the reproduction of the queen, some of whose offspring will have a chance to found new colonies. Similarly, the social system constituted by the cells of an animal is one where, in general, each somatic cell works not for its own benefit but for the survival of the whole animal and for the reproductive success of the animal. One could say that, in complex animals, things are organized in this way: "from each cell according to its abilities, to each cell according to its needs"; and in a eusocial colony, they are organized in this way: "from each colony member according to its abilities, to each colony member according to its needs."[46]

However, the cells in a body and the members in a colony can be said to receive according to their needs only if their needs are narrowly defined in terms of the contribution that each cell or each colony member makes to the association as a whole.[47] Neither organisms nor superorganisms are cooperative systems where "the free development of each is the condition for the free development of all." In fact, they are the opposite of that: the free development of each threatens the unity of the whole and is therefore something to be curbed and suppressed. There is no "realm of freedom" to be found within the "associated producers" of life in an organism or in a superorganism. Contrary to Wilson's suggestion, you will not find Marxian communism in eusocial species; likewise, you will not find it inside the human body, in the way its cells interact with each other. The fact that human nature is not eusocial and that humanity is not a superorgranism does not in any way show that we are the "wrong species" for Marxian communism. The path to eusociality and the path to Marxian communism are different paths.[48]

2

Transformation

Natura Pura

In his *Discourse on the Origin and Basis of Inequality among Men*, Jean-Jacques Rousseau presents his views on the state of nature. As we have seen, for Hobbes the state of nature is the absence of a sovereign power. For Rousseau, humans in the state of nature are humans without civilization, and there are elements of what Rousseau takes to be "civilization" that precede government. Significantly, Hobbes's humans in the state of nature have language, whereas Rousseau's do not. According to Rousseau, in order to understand what the "pure state of nature" consists in, one needs to conduct a thought experiment that involves "stripping" humans "of all the artificial faculties"—language being one of them.[1] We need to subtract in thought all the elements and components of civilization from the human modes of life with which we are familiar. Rousseau argues that once we make this subtraction, we can see that "the savage lives within himself; sociable man, always outside himself."[2] Humans in the state of nature have a "solitary way of life."[3]

Rousseau refers to some "barbarous and savage" populations, like the "Hottentots" and the "Caribs—which of all existing peoples has thus far moved away the least from the state of nature."[4] These populations are close to the "first," "genuine," or "pure" state of nature, but they also have elements of civilization: they have linguistic communication, they have families, small communities, tools, etc. In contrast, humans in the "first state of nature" do not have "any kind of relations" with one another.[5] Humans in this prelinguistic state of nature might sometime bump into each other, but they do not interact in ways that could be described as social. Men and women meet "fortuitously" to satisfy their sexual urges, but they ignore each other after sexual intercourse, and they might not even recognize each other if they meet again. In the state of nature, mothers stop interacting with their children as soon as the children can survive without their help, which is not long after birth, according to Rousseau.[6]

The solitary mode of life that Rousseau attributes to humans in this "genuine" state of nature is much less "social" than the one found in Hobbes's "naturall condition." Rousseau's state of nature is a minimally social mode of life, one of peaceful coexistence:

> Savage man, once he has eaten, is at peace with all of nature and the friend of all his fellow humans. Is it sometimes a question of contending for his meal? He never comes to blows without having first compared the difficulty of prevailing with that of finding his subsistence elsewhere. And as pride is not involved in the fight, it ends with a few blows; the victor eats, the vanquished goes off to try his luck, and all is at peace. [...] Since savage man desires only the things he knows and knows only those things whose possession is in his power or are easily acquired, nothing should be so tranquil as his soul and nothing so limited as his mind.[7]

Rousseau claims that "man is naturally good" and that "savages are not evil precisely because they do not know what it is to be good."[8] He argues that "man in his primitive state" is "gentle" and "restrained by natural pity from doing harm to anyone."[9]

Rousseau also says that it does not matter whether his reconstruction is historically accurate; he concedes that he does not have enough evidence for historical accuracy. What matters is being able to grasp the differences between the state of nature and the state of civilization. For Hobbes, the state of nature is a constant shadow and a constant threat. In contrast, for Rousseau, the mode of life of humans in the original state of nature is not only peacefully uncooperative but also inaccessible to civilized humans. It might be possible for some to return to simpler (less sophisticated) modes of life than those found in the most developed nations. But humans with some degree of civilization are forever transformed and do not have access to the original state of nature:

> It is the spirit of society alone and the inequality it engenders that so changes and alters all our natural inclinations.[10]

Humans left the state of nature because, unlike other animals, they have "the faculty of perfecting" themselves and their conditions of life.[11] This natural faculty has led to the emergence of various artificial faculties, including the linguistic ones. This, in turn, has allowed us to make our own history, and the history we have made has resulted in unintended and irreversible changes. Departing from more "primitive" modes of life was "a fatal accident."[12] It involved various steps, including the emergence of language, families, communities, agriculture, metallurgy, private property, governments, and laws. While the other animals do not make their own history and thus cannot change their own nature, human "perfectibility" alters human nature.

Rousseau, commenting on reports about orangutans and their solitary modes of life, tentatively suggests that these human-like creatures living in remote forests might actually be humans in the state of nature. They could be perfectible beings who have not experienced the series of "accidents" that have led other populations to develop increasingly complex forms of civilization. On this view, orangutan modes of life, despite being nonlinguistic and minimally social, are human modes of life.[13]

Rousseau emphasizes that original natural inequalities are relatively minor and harmless, while the inequalities created by civilization, and the forms of oppression resulting from such inequalities, are not. He proposes that, if these artificial inequalities continue to grow, everything "will be swallowed up by the monster" of unfreedom, leading to "a new state of nature, different from the one with which we began, in that the first was the state of nature in its purity and this last is the fruit of an excess in corruption." In this new hyper-corrupt and hyper-impure state of nature, where "everything is brought back to the sole law of the stronger," the "contract of government" is dissolved and "the uprising that ends with a sultan being strangled or dethroned is as lawful an act as those by which, the day before, he disposed of his subjects' lives and goods."[14] Thus, for Rousseau, the Hobbesian war of all against all is a possibility and a threat, but not as a result of unchanging human dispositions. It is a threat that stems from the human "constitution" brought about by civilization.

*

Philosophical theorizing about human nature often seeks to "*change*" the world, not just to describe or interpret it.[15] Such theorizing often expresses views about what modes of life ought to be pursued or avoided. Hobbes and Rousseau were influenced by and involved in the political events of their own times, and the political conflicts that structured those events. The specific historical details are complex.[16] But, in any case, Hobbes depicted the "naturall condition" as war of all against all in order to persuade his contemporaries to embrace political arrangements that he considered advantageous; and Rousseau portrayed the peaceful, solitary life of "man" in the "pure state of nature" as part of an attack on institutions and social arrangements that he experienced and detested. Both Hobbes and Rousseau considered modes of life that differed from those they could observe in the societies in which they lived. Their views, along with various interpretations and misinterpretations of such views, have had and continue to have a profound influence on human lives.

Natura Lapsa

According to Rousseau, human nature is shaped by the unintended consequences of human actions.[17] This idea can be traced back to the second and third chapters of Genesis. In Genesis 3, we are told that Eve ("the woman") and then Adam ("the man") contravene God's command. The command in question is the one that God gives to Adam in Genesis 2: "of the tree of the knowledge of good and evil you shall not eat, for in the day that you eat of it you shall die."[18] This interaction occurs just before God creates Eve. According to God, "it is not good that the man should be alone; I will make him a helper as his partner."[19] This suggests that initially the social relation between the man and the woman is, at least to some extent, non-hierarchical.

In Genesis 3, after encouragement from the serpent, Eve eats the fruit of the tree of knowledge. She then gives some to Adam, who eats it too.[20] God responds by banishing Adam and Eve from the garden. God tells the woman that, from now on, her husband will "rule" over her and that she will have to submit to his authority.[21] This does not necessarily involve a change in the woman's nature, only a change in her social relations. But God also tells Eve: "I will make your pangs in childbirth exceedingly great; in pain you shall bring forth children."[22] One plausible interpretation is that there is a change in Eve's corporeal nature, at least in relation to pregnancy-related processes—a change that Eve transmits to all her female descendants. Adam and his male descendants will also suffer, but only because the non-Edenic "ground," says God, is "cursed." They will have to toil in order to provide for themselves and their families—the Edenic bounty will be inaccessible.[23] Thus, in Adam's case, the problems will derive not from a change in his corporeal nature, but from the fact that he—and all his descendants—will have to live outside the garden, where conditions are hard. There will be suffering in biological reproduction (possibly resulting from a change in the woman's body) and suffering in economic production (due to an environmental change, a change in the external conditions of life).

Another thing to note is that, immediately after eating the forbidden fruit, Adam and Eve realize that they are naked and sew fig leaves together to cover their genitals.[24] This suggests that, before eating the fruit, Adam and Eve relate to their bodies like non-human animals do, with no awareness of their nakedness. The ingested knowledge changes this, for them and their descendants. It could be argued that this change in the way one relates to one's own body, which scares Adam and makes him want to hide,[25] constitutes a change in human nature. Alternatively, it could be argued that acquiring knowledge of good and evil is in itself a change in human nature.

In Genesis 2, God tells Adam that he may eat freely from any of the trees of the garden except the tree of knowledge, and that he will "surely die" if he eats from that tree.[26] However, as predicted by the serpent, Adam does not die when he eats the forbidden fruit; he will die many years later. In Genesis 3, when He talks to Adam after the fruit has been eaten, God tells Adam that he is "dust" and that he will revert to being "dust."[27] God asserts that "the man has become like one of us" in that he now knows good and evil, and were Adam to eat the fruit of the tree of life, he would "live forever," something that God wants to avoid.[28] On one reading of the text, Adam is created (at least potentially) immortal; he becomes mortal by eating from the tree of knowledge (an act which corrupts his corporeal nature) and he could in principle become immortal again by eating from the tree of life. On another reading, Adam is created mortal; he could live forever by eating from the tree of life, which is not forbidden, but this possibility is taken away from him when he leaves the garden. On this second interpretation, Adam remains mortal throughout all the events narrated in Genesis 2 and 3. The thing that changes is his access to something that gives eternal life.[29]

In any case, what emerges from the biblical text is the idea that humans start making their own history when they eat from the tree of knowledge. It is at that moment that humans become genuinely historical beings.

*

Paul of Tarsus calls Adam's action a "transgression" and a "sin." These are terms that do not appear in Genesis 2 and 3.[30] In Romans, Paul asserts that "sin came into the world through one man, and death came through sin", and that "death spread to all" because "all have sinned."[31] Humans lack access to eternal life as a result of Adam's actions. But how can it be the case that "through one man [...] all have sinned"? The most influential answer to this question is given by Augustine of Hippo, who claims that, in a sense, all sinned in Adam:

> The particular form in which we were to live as individuals had not been created and distributed to us; but the seminal nature from which we were to be propagated already existed. And, when this was vitiated by sin and bound by the chain of death and justly condemned, man could not be born of man in any other condition.[32]

According to the Church Father, sin and death are currently unavoidable because we all sinned in Adam's germline. Due to Adam's transgression, all humans are creatures whose will has been vitiated and who are thereby unable to choose and act as they should. The "quality of the human will" has been compromised. This *natura lapsa* is the outcome of Edenic humans damaging the pristine human nature that God had created:

> On that day their nature was indeed changed for the worse and vitiated.[33]

Adam's *original sin* is a sin that originates all sin, both phylogenetically and ontogenetically. Augustine maintains that it is because of Adam's transgression that the reproductive organs are not under voluntary control. The transgression weakened the human ability to control one's body, with the result that one's body parts can now disobey one's will:

> When the first man transgressed the law of God, he began to have another law in his members which was repugnant to the law of his mind, and he felt the evil of his own disobedience when he experienced in the disobedience of his flesh a most righteous retribution recoiling on himself. Such, then, was "the opening of his eyes" which the serpent had promised him in his temptation—the knowledge, in fact, of something which he had better been ignorant of. Then, indeed, did man perceive within himself what he had done; then did he distinguish evil from good—not by avoiding it, but by enduring it. For it certainly was not just that obedience should be rendered by his servant, that is, his body, to him, who had not obeyed his own Lord. Well, then, how significant is the fact that the eyes, and lips, and tongue, and hands, and feet, and the bending of back, and neck, and sides, are all placed within our power—to be applied to such operations as are suitable to them, when we have a body free from impediments and in a sound state of health; but when it must come to man's great function of the procreation of children the members which were expressly created for this purpose will not obey the direction of the will, but lust has to be waited for to set these members in motion, as if it had legal right over them, and sometimes it refuses to act when the mind wills, while often it acts against its will! Must not this bring the blush of shame over the freedom of the human will, that by its contempt of God, its own Commander, it has

> lost all proper command for itself over its own members? Now, wherein could be found a more fitting demonstration of the just depravation of human nature by reason of its disobedience, than in the disobedience of those parts whence nature herself derives subsistence by succession?[34]

Augustine suggests that, before being thrown out of the garden, Adam could control his erections and decide when to have one and when not to have one. It is for this reason that, before his transgression, Adam did not feel the need to hide his genitals. Before the transgression, sexual organs and sexual intercourse were not sources of shame since they were under voluntary control. It is the sudden lack of control, and the vulnerability that comes with it, which causes Adam to feel shame and fear.[35] Had Adam not eaten the forbidden fruit, the voluntary control of the penis would have been retained in him and all his descendants.[36]

Some body parts are more disobedient than others, but the loss of control is a general one. Aging, illness, and death are themselves due to a human will that has become unable to control the body:

> Man's very mind, and even his lower part, his flesh, do not obey his will. Even against his will his mind is often troubled; and his flesh endures pain, grows old, and dies, and suffers all manner of things which we should not suffer against our will if our nature were in every way and in all its parts obedient to our will. For, now, the flesh is in such a condition that it simply cannot serve our will.[37]

This loss of control also means that lust, which did not exist in prelapsarian humans, is now involved in every act of human reproduction. Unlike prelapsarian humans, postlapsarian humans can only reproduce by sinning.[38] We are the slaves of lust, and carnal concupiscence contributes to the cross-generational reoccurrence of our postlapsarian condition:

> The cause of evil [in infants] is not their being born of the union of bodies, since, even if human nature had not been vitiated by the sin of the first man, children could not have been generated except from the union of bodies. The reason those born of the union of bodies are under the power of the Devil [...] is that they are born through that concupiscence by which the flesh lusts against the spirit and forces the spirit to lust against the flesh.[39]

Infants, before they can perform any actions, are "under the power of the Devil." Those who happen to die before being baptized will not be able to access God's grace; only the Church can provide access to salvation.[40]

Augustine criticizes those who believe that the sacraments are not necessary for salvation. He also criticizes those who believe that the sacraments can be invalidated by people's actions, including the sins of those who administer them. He argues against those, such as the Pelagians, who maintain that humans can find within themselves, by their own free will, the path to salvation. The Church is the necessary and uniquely legitimate intermediary between humans and Christ. In the garden, Adam had access to God's grace; in the postlapsarian world, God's grace cannot be directly accessed, even by children. The garden has been lost and God is distant. Christ's death offers a way to access divine grace again, but only via the Church.

Augustine wanted to persuade his contemporaries that they had to submit to the authority of the Church, and that children had to be brought under such authority too. He aimed at encouraging modes of life that fully recognized the authority of the Church. Augustine's ideas on human nature, and his reading of Paul's claims on Adam, became influential in ways that no one could have anticipated. Many within the Christian tradition invoked and adopted these ideas. Many suggested amendments and additions.[41] In the West, these ideas, over the centuries, penetrated, explicitly or implicitly, directly or indirectly, into most conversations and decisions about feasible and infeasible social arrangements, and about desirable and undesirable ways of doing things. These ideas had a profound impact on Western social institutions and social practices and, through the subsequent influence of the West on the rest of the globe, they had an impact on the human species in its entirety.

The loss of paradise, and specifically Augustine's way of thinking about this loss, has been said to constitute "the original mythologeme of Western culture, a sort of originary traumatism that has profoundly marked Christian and modern culture, condemning to failure every search for happiness on earth."[42] The practical impact of ideas about human nature that manage to become influential, or even hegemonic (to use the Gramscian term), can extend far beyond the immediate practical aims of those who initially put forward the ideas in question. In some cases, it can last for centuries.

Regnum

The pessimistic Augustinian view of human nature is often said to have influenced Hobbes.[43] In a general sense, this is undoubtedly true. However, there are some differences between the Augustinian and the Hobbesian view that are worth noting, especially when considering the impact of ideas about human nature on human praxis.

In his writings on "liberty," Hobbes asserts that there is nothing metaphysically distinctive about the human will: it is determined in the same way that everything else is. The human will can be free only in the sense that (and to the extent that) there are no obstacles in the causal path linking the will to actions and behaviors. But the process of deliberation itself is not free from necessity. According to Hobbes, a will that is free from necessity is unintelligible.[44] In having a will that is not free from necessity, we are like the other animals. We possess linguistic abilities that the other animals lack, which allow us to connect our thoughts, build collective memories, and impose complex rules onto our thinking processes. We also have hands that permit the construction of tools. However, language and hands do not make us metaphysically superior to the other animals.[45]

In his debates with Hobbes, Bishop John Bramhall proposes various arguments against the Hobbesian view. Bramhall is in favor of a version of the traditional scholastic notion of *liberum arbitrium*. The argument that interests us here is the argument concerning the Fall. Bramhall claims that if Hobbes is right, Adam's actions in the garden were not the result of a free choice. According to Bramhall, this carries blasphemous implications:

> He [Hobbes] makes Adam to have had no liberty from necessity before his fall, yea he proceeds so far, as to affirm, that all humane wills, his and ours, and each propension of our wills, even during

> our deliberation, are as much necessitated as anything else whatsoever; that we have no more power to forbear those actions which we do, than the fire hath power not to burn. Though I honour T.H. for his person and for his learning, yet I must confess ingenuously, I hate this doctrine from my heart. And I believe both I have reason so to do, and all others who shall seriously ponder the horrid consequences which flow from it. It destroys liberty, and dishonours the nature of man. [...] It makes the first cause, that is, God Almighty, to be the introducer of all evil and sin into the world.[46]

Hobbes responds that Adam's actions and choices were indeed "necessitated," but denies that this carries blasphemous implications. Adam's actions and choices occurred in accordance with God's plan, although they went against God's command. According to Hobbes, the sole purpose of the Fall was to teach Adam that the operation of the will is not free from necessity:

> These words *Hast thou eaten of the tree whereof I commanded that thou shouldest not eat*, convince Adam that, notwithstanding God had placed him in the Garden a means to keep him perpetually from dying in case he should accommodate his will to obedience of God's commandment concerning the tree of knowledge of good and evil, yet Adam was not so much master of his own will as to do it. Whereby is signified, that a mortal man, though invited by the promise of immortality, cannot govern his own will, though his will govern his actions; which dependence of the actions on the will, is that which properly and truly is called *liberty*.[47]

By leaving Eden, Adam lost access to the tree of eternal life, but his nature was not affected. According to Hobbes, Adam and Eve "were not immortal by their creation."[48] There were no Fall-related changes in human bodies: the departure from Eden did not change anything in human corporeality; it did not change anything in relation to the human will either. The Augustinian idea that the Fall degraded human nature—that it weakened the human will and thereby made the body disobedient—is absent in Hobbes: the problems that affect human life are not due to the corrupting impact of the Fall.[49]

What Hobbes says about Adam and the Fall has implications for his views on salvation. According to the Augustinian tradition, after the Last Judgment, humans will be restored to their prelapsarian state; they will be "restored to incorruption" due to God's grace repairing the damage done by the Fall.[50] In fact, humans will acquire a condition that is better (more "glorious") than that enjoyed by Adam in the garden. Those who can enter God's Kingdom will regain access to eternal life, and this access will not be fragile, as it was for Adam in the garden. The will of the elect (and therefore their capacity not to sin and to be moved by what is right) will acquire its perfect (lust-free) form. Mistakes like that made by Adam in the garden will not happen again, and there will not be a second Fall. Humans will again become ahistorical and no return to history will be possible.[51]

Some elements of this Augustinian narrative are present in Hobbes's texts, but, according to the English philosopher, the elect will not gain access to eternal life by reacquiring uncorrupted bodies. Rather, they will gain access to eternal life by being admitted to the "new Tree of Life," Christ.[52] Moreover, there will not be a reversal to an uncorrupted, better-functioning will. Adam never had a will that he could control arbitrarily, and there cannot be a return to such a free will; nor can there be a transition toward a form of will control that is better than the one Adam had when he sinned in the garden.

Hobbes claims that the Kingdom of God "is a reall, not a metaphoricall Kingdome."[53] He distinguishes between the old Kingdom of God and the New Kingdom of God. The old one was

God's reign over "His Peculiar People"; it was "cast off by the rebellion of the Israelites in the election of Saul." The "restored" Kingdom of God will come about through a "New Covenant," that is, the pact between Jesus and those who believe that He is the Christ.[54] The New Kingdom will be on Earth, and it will be "a Civil Common-wealth."[55] It will involve the resurrection of human bodies and will be eternal, but it will only occur with Jesus's second coming.[56] In this "World to come," all human kingdoms—all kingdoms with a human sovereign power—will vanish.[57]

Hobbes says that the Leviathan is a "Mortall God, to which we owe under the Immortal God, our peace and defence."[58] The Leviathan will be swept away by Christ, who, as "Lieutenant of God," will be the head of a new political body constituted by the assembly of the faithful.[59] From a political viewpoint, the contrast between the present world and the world to come is striking. In the present world, there is no social unity in the absence of a sovereign power, no political body, only a "disunited" multitude of individual bodies fearful of each other. Even with a sovereign power present, there is a constant risk of falling into the all-against-all mode of life. The forms of cooperation that are possible in present-world commonwealths are much more stable than those found in the state of nature, but the state of nature remains part of present-world commonwealths in the form of a constant threat of dissolution through civil war.[60] Until Jesus's second coming, the state—identified by Hobbes with the biblical sea monster that embodies the forces of evil—will be needed.[61]

The threat of dissolution will disappear in the New Kingdom, but not through a return to a pristine human nature. Human nature does not change, according to the Hobbesian line of argument. How and why will the possibility of political and cooperative dissolution disappear? Perhaps in the New Kingdom—which given God's resources is a post-scarcity environment—there will be enough to make sure that no "two men desire the same thing, which nevertheless they cannot both enjoy." This would require not just abundance but also a general way of coordinating people's wants (to avoid any two individuals having desires with incompatible satisfaction conditions). Once the New Kingdom is established, the elect will want what is good for the Christ-headed commonwealth in the same way that the bees and the ants want what is good for their colony. But if so, how? Perhaps the human members of this community will want what is good for the collective thanks to the immense pheromonal power of God's Grace, which will affect people's minds but not change the way they operate. Alternatively, and more simply, the New Kingdom will be without conflict because it will offer eternal life, which in turn will remove any fear of death and any reason to criticize social arrangements. When eternal life becomes frictionlessly available, nothing else is needed to ensure unity. With Christ-assured eternal life, and the fear gone, the state of nature will immediately vanish and, with it, the Leviathan—there will be no need to wait for it to "wither away."

*

Ideas about perfect forms of human cooperation are linked to ideas about human nature, and they can profoundly affect human praxis. Let us briefly revisit Rousseau, Marx, and Engels.

On Rousseau's account, the faculty of perfecting oneself, which humans have due to their free will, has cumulatively and unintentionally modified human nature. We could say that, for Rousseau, human nature has been changed via human niche construction. These unintentional modifications have led to various problems of unfreedom that were absent in the state of nature. These problems of unfreedom ought to be resolved, but we cannot deal with them by trying to return to the state of nature. In his works after the second *Discourse*, Rousseau suggests that it might be possible to use our perfectibility to solve, at least partially, some of the problems that such perfectibility has generated. He explores ways of resolving these problems through political praxis, through education, and in private forms.

As for Marx and Engels, it would certainly be useful to have a detailed description of the "true realm of freedom," an account of modes of life that allow "the free development of each [to be] the condition for the free development of all." The two German revolutionaries said little about what full communism would involve. Toward the end of his life, Marx read Lewis H. Morgan's work on "ancient societies" and Iroquois social arrangements. After Marx's death, Engels used Marx's notes to write his own book on the origins of the family, the state, and private property.

According to Morgan, humans can move—and are indeed moving—toward a "higher plane of society," which consists in a "revival, in a higher form, of the liberty, equality, and fraternity" found in ancestral populations.[62] The suggestion, endorsed by Marx and Engels, is that ancestral humans had a form of egalitarianism that was then lost as a result of intricate cultural, political, and economic dynamics. In the future, we will be able to return to something resembling the ancestral condition, although the new condition will also be better: it will be possible to access a "higher" (communist) mode of life. Engels suggests that the process taking us from primitive small-scale tribal communism to universal large-scale communism will involve various changes in our mutable human nature. Should this new Kingdom come, it will be through praxis and through a social reorganization that, says Engels, will allow us to put the state "into a museum"—much like we would do with the fossilized remains of an extinct Leviathan-like sea monster.[63]

Whether narratives like these should be elements of future human praxis (and if so, in what form) remains an open question.

3

Subordination

Slaves and Women

Ideas about human nature can have profound impacts when they gain widespread acceptance and become diffusely embedded in society, or when powerful social agents adopt them. In some cases, the impacts are relatively superficial and short-lived; in other cases, they are deep and longlasting. In some cases, the impacts are direct; in others, they are tortuously indirect. In some cases, the impacts are immediate; in others, they are delayed.

Apart from Augustine's, another view of human nature that has had a longlasting influence is obviously Aristotle's. According to him, the full exercise of a certain kind of rationality in the context of the *polis* is necessary in order to be fully human. Aristotle considers those who are "by nature and not merely by fortune citiless" (because they lack the drive to associate with others in *polis*-like ways) as less than fully human. But he also makes distinctions among those who have this drive and are able to express it within the *polis*: not all of them are fully rational, and thus not all of them are political in the highest degree. Those who are "slaves by nature" lack the relevant kind of deliberative rationality: they lack a component of the rational soul. Women, excluding those who are also natural slaves, possess the part of the rational soul that those who are slaves by nature lack. However, in women, this part exists in a weaker form:

> There are by nature various classes of rulers and ruled. For the free rules the slave, the male the female, and the man the child in a different way. And all possess the various parts of the soul, but possess them in different ways; for the slave has not got the deliberative part at all, and the female has it, but without full authority [*akuron*], while the child has it, but in an undeveloped form.[1]

While the male children of free adults do eventually develop full rationality, women and natural slaves do not. Women and natural slaves are human but not fully so. They are lacking in comparison with the ideal (most complete, fully developed) type.

Those who are slaves by nature may be free in practice, if they have not been enslaved by anyone, but they ought to be enslaved. Being enslaved is beneficial to them. According to Aristotle, most "barbarians" (non-Greeks) are slaves by nature. This is shown by their savage ways of behaving. Those who are slaves by nature are not identifiable from the way they look, but they can be detected through their verbal and nonverbal behavior, which reveals something about their inferior minds.[2] Natural slaves differ from non-human animals in that they possess some capacity to participate in reason or, at the very least, to recognize and respond to it. Given that they do not possess reason fully, however, they can make their contribution to a *polis* only by serving their masters. Slaves are "tools."[3] A group of slaves cannot form a *polis*.[4]

Women are also, by their nature, excluded from high-level political activity, according to Aristotle. Within the household, the wife has authority, but it is a partial authority subjected to the higher authority of the husband. Women's minds lack the kind of completeness that can be found in free men. Women have an important role to play within the political community, but a subordinate role.[5]

Women and slaves have roles within the polis that, in certain respects, parallel the subordinate roles of drones and worker bees in a hive.[6] Aristotle's political motivations, especially those for his views on slavery, are difficult to reconstruct.[7] Independent of Aristotle's own political agenda, Aristotelian ideas on these matters had far-reaching impacts that went beyond his aims and intentions.

Slaves and Colonies

The Aristotelian notion of natural slavery was invoked in sixteenth-century disputes about the treatment of the Indigenous populations in the Spanish colonies in America. The most important of such disputes was the Valladolid debate (1550–1), with the main participants being Dominican friar and Bishop Bartolomé de Las Casas and jurist and humanist scholar Juan Ginés de Sepúlveda.[8]

Sepúlveda argued that the "Caribs" and the "Indians" were natural slaves in the Aristotelian sense.[9] He believed it was right to wage war against these people, expropriate their belongings, and enslave them. Although the "Indians" were free before the Spaniards' arrival, Sepúlveda claimed that they had been natural slaves all along. He characterized the "Indians" as possessing "natural rudeness and inferiority." This inferiority was demonstrated by their "sins against nature," such as "the incredible sacrifices of human beings, their horrible banquets of human flesh, and their impious worship of idols."[10] According to Sepúlveda:

> [These people] require, by their own nature and in their own interests, to be placed under the authority of civilized and virtuous princes or nations […]. Compare […] those blessings enjoyed by Spaniards of prudence, genius, magnanimity, temperance, humanity, and religion with those of the *homunculi* in whom you will scarcely find even vestiges of humanity, who not only possess no science but who also lack letters […]. Neither do they have written laws, but barbaric institutions and customs. They do not even have private property.[11]
>
> These barbarians of the New World […] are as inferior to the Spaniards as are children to adults and women to men. The difference between them is as great as between a wild, cruel people

> and the most merciful, between the grossly intemperate and the most continent and temperate, and, I am tempted to say, between men and monkeys.[12]

Sepúlveda, who never traveled to the Americas, faced harsh criticism from Las Casas, who by 1550 had spent decades in the New World denouncing and opposing the *encomienda* forced-labor system. Las Casas has been said to be "one of the first American anthropologists."[13] He sought to study and understand human differences as facets of a common humanity:

> [These people] are not ignorant, inhuman, or bestial. Rather, long before they had heard the word Spaniard, they had properly organized states, wisely ordered by excellent laws, religion, and custom. They cultivated friendship and, bound together in common fellowship, lived in populous cities in which they wisely administered the affairs of both peace and war justly and equitably, truly governed by laws that at very many points surpass ours, and could have won the admiration of the sages of Athens.[14]
>
> Mankind is one, and all men are alike in that which concerns their creation and all natural things [. . .] No one is born enlightened.[15]
>
> [I intend] to liberate my own Spanish nation from the error and very grave and very pernicious illusion in which they now live and have always lived, of considering these people to lack the essential characteristics of men, judging them brute beasts incapable of virtue and religion, depreciating their good qualities and exaggerating the bad which is in them.[16]

Sylvia Wynter argues that Las Casas should not be considered an innovator. Las Casas's view had its roots in the old Christian idea that all humans are born equal, equally flawed but also able, at least in principle, to get closer and gain access to divine grace.[17] Sepúlveda's humanist view, influenced by the Aristotelian texts, replaced the idea of a Church-certified ranking of spiritual perfection with a new ranking (not controlled by the Church) based on rational faculties.[18]

The rationality-centered humanist perspective allowed Sepúlveda and others to argue that the Indigenous populations of the Americas (as well as other non-European peoples) were rational but only to a lesser degree, justifying treatment that would have been illegitimate if applied to European populations. According to Wynter, rational perfection/imperfection replaced spiritual perfection/imperfection as a hierarchical criterion. She also asserts that views about degrees of rationality became linked to racial classification: in this context, discourses about racial inferiority emerged as discourses about the inferior rationality of non-Europeans. Aristotle's ideas on natural slavery contributed to shaping the forms of racism that became widespread with European colonial expansion. The suggestion is that, in the last few hundred years, discussions about human equality have occurred within the hierarchical and exclusionary framework that the sixteenth-century humanists adopted (and adapted) from Aristotle.[19]

Wynter's historico-philosophical reconstruction raises complex questions that cannot be discussed here. Nonetheless, the hypothesis that an important transition occurred at the time of the encounter between European settlers and Indigenous peoples of America is a plausible one. This transition had at its core the link between ideas on human nature and various forms of transformative praxis. An important aspect of this transition revolved around the question of who had the authority to rank humans, and according to what standards. In this transition, which has shaped global history over the last 500 years, the Aristotelian views on natural slavery (and on rationality as necessary for being fully human) played a crucial role.

Part Two

4

Essentialism

Sciences and Channels

Nowadays, just like in the past, ideas about human nature are invoked in relation to—and in attempts to settle—politically controversial matters. One way of intervening in current debates on human nature is by engaging with recent philosophical discussions of the *concept* (or *notion*, or *conception*) of human nature. These are discussions aimed at identifying, comparing, and assessing general ways of thinking about human nature. Focusing on relatively abstract ways of thinking can be useful as it allows for a broader, though not disinterested or pure, perspective.[1]

Arguably, a general way of thinking about human nature is a general way of thinking about what we fundamentally are, or at least some aspects of it. Aristotle, for instance, maintains that among our fundamental features are the linguistic and reasoning abilities that "by nature" enable some of us to cooperate in intensely political ways; and he claims that "by nature" there are some fundamental differences between men and women, between free citizens and slaves, and between members of the *polis* and those who are "citiless." Augustine argues that one of our fundamental traits is the corruption that we brought upon ourselves—upon our "nature"—as a result of violating God's command in the garden, a corruption that only Christ can (and will) wipe out; this corruption involves, among other things, an inability to control one's will and one's genitals. According to Hobbes, among the things that are fundamental about us are our corporeal and mental equality (which "Nature hath made"), as well as those "natural" dispositions that, in the absence of a sovereign power and of a guarantee of eternal life, result in a state of constant mutual fear. And so on.

In today's epistemic circumstances, a good way of thinking about what we fundamentally are ought to be informed by well-supported scientific findings and theories about humans and their relations to their biotic and abiotic surroundings. This can (and should) be accepted even by those who, for whatever reason, believe that what we fundamentally are cannot be captured entirely, in all its aspects, by scientific discourses. The suggestion is that the sciences are imperfect but reliable sources of information about (some aspects of) what we fundamentally are.

Scientific discourses about humans are imperfect not only because our knowledge-producing strategies are fallible and limited in general ways, but also because contemporary experts in this area (just like Aristotle, Augustine, Hobbes, Rousseau, and Marx) are not disinterested and passive observers. They are active participants in the web of social conflicts. The more some ideas are likely to have an impact on systemic elements of the human social niche, the more these ideas, and the controversies surrounding them, are important nodes in the web of social conflicts. This applies to all ideas produced by our cooperating minds, whether they are labeled "scientific," "artistic," "political," or in some other way. But influential scientific ideas are embedded in the web of social conflicts in distinctive ways. Individuals and social groups often attempt to direct and control scientific discourses and scientific theorizing—including the direction of scientific research—in order to promote and protect their own economic and noneconomic interests. This, however, is compatible with scientific research playing a distinctive knowledge-producing role within human praxis, and is partly due to the world-transforming powers of the tools that scientific research generates. A proper explanation of these world-transforming powers cannot ignore the ways in which science partially (and not only partisanly) captures the structures of reality within its discourses.

Timpanaro suggests that we ought to appropriate the sciences that are normally considered "natural" and use them to give content and structure to our view of what we fundamentally are. These sciences generate not only world-transforming instruments but also ways of understanding the limits of our transformative efforts and, more generally, our "place" in the universe. Theories and observations about the ways we are similar to and different from each other, similar to and different from other living beings, and similar to and different from nonliving physical entities have always played a role in the elaboration of ideas about our "nature." The natural sciences offer us good tools for understanding all these similarities and differences.[2]

Alongside considering the current role of science, it should be acknowledged that ideas about what we fundamentally are can have an impact on our modes of life. Present modes of life are partly the outcome of the work of past human praxis, including past conversations and decisions about which ways of living together and doing things collectively ought to be conserved, modified, pursued, avoided, and so on. This, in turn, means that present modes of life are partly the result of ideas about human nature that influenced past praxis. Future modes of life will be conditioned by present praxis, and thus also by the ideas about human nature influencing our current conversations and decisions. Ideas about human nature affect human praxis by interacting in complex ways with many other cultural and non-cultural factors and operate in a constantly evolving context. But this complexity does not make them less important.

We can articulate the role of ideas about human nature in human praxis with the help of a metaphor: a general way of thinking about human nature serves as a *channel of communication* between, on the one hand, ideas about what we fundamentally are (or at least some aspects of it) and, on the other, thoughts and actions that directly or indirectly shape our modes of life. The existence of this communication channel means that asking what a good concept of human nature looks like requires asking how this communication channel could and should operate. A good way of thinking about human nature needs to work well as a communication channel in this sense. In today's context, this also means that a good concept of human nature should function adequately as a communication channel between, on the one hand, scientifically well-supported ideas about what we fundamentally are—especially those emanating from the more "natural" sciences—and, on the other hand, conversations and decisions about our modes of life.[3]

Darwin's Barnacles

An intuitively plausible general way of thinking about human nature is this: human nature is an essence. This is the *nature-as-essence* way of thinking about human nature, or the *essentialist concept* of human nature. What kind of thing could the human essence be? On a standard view, the human essence is a bundle of properties that all and only humans have. The properties in the bundle are individually necessary and jointly sufficient for being human.[4] It is in virtue of having this bundle of properties that each human is human. What kind of properties are in the bundle? One possible answer is that the invariant bundle is a bundle of phenotypic traits. Phenotypic traits are the morphological, physiological, neural, psychological, behavioral, and social features (or "characters," to use Darwin's term) of biological organisms. On a view like this, the human essence can overlap with the essence of other species. Having four limbs and the ability to feel emotions such as fear and joy might be essential (necessary) phenotypic characteristics of both humans and chimpanzees. However, there are traits that are essential for being human and that chimpanzees do not have (and vice versa). The human-essence bundle and the chimpanzee-essence bundle share some components, but not all.

Once this way of thinking about these matters is embraced, one can begin elaborating a full-fledged account of human nature by trying to determine which phenotypic traits are actually part of the human essence and which are not. However, this way of thinking about human nature is inconsistent with what we know about biological species. It is inconsistent with Darwin's discoveries about biological variation.

Darwin spent eight years of his life (from 1846 to 1854) studying barnacles.[5] Barnacles are sessile marine animals. They are crustaceans, related to crabs and lobsters. Darwin spent eight years observing barnacles because he wanted to understand biological variation, and he could find a lot of variation in barnacles. The key lesson that he drew from his long study is this:

> Not only does every external character vary greatly in most of the species, but the internal parts very often vary to a surprising degree [...] I must express my deliberate conviction that it is hopeless to find in any species [...] any one part or organ [...] absolutely invariable in form or structure.[6]

After devoting eight years to these "lowly" creatures, Darwin decided that he was "unwilling to spend more time on the subject."[7] But the study of biological variation remained one of his obsessions. Throughout his life, he never stopped collecting, recording, measuring, and classifying biological variants in form, structure, and behavior.[8]

Variation is ubiquitous because new variants or modifications appear all the time, and some of these modifications are passed from one generation to the next. This is what Darwin calls *descent with modification*. He did not know much about the mechanisms and processes responsible for the emergence and cross-generational transmission of new variants. He had views on these matters that turned out to be incorrect.[9] However, the idea that biological variation is ubiquitous, that it is constantly renewed, and that some variation reoccurs trans-generationally has been overwhelmingly confirmed and is at the core of the contemporary evolutionary understanding of biological organisms. Kim Sterelny writes:

> Beginning with Darwin, and with even greater emphasis in more recent evolutionary theory, evolutionary biology has taught us that species are typically variable at a time, that they change over time, and that there is no principled bound on the variation to be found in a species at a time, or over time.[10]

Darwin's lifelong interest in variation contributed to his discovery of selection processes, which in turn fueled his interest in variation. He understood how selection dynamics (natural selection, as well as artificial and sexual selection) could explain the wonderfully diversified traits of biological organisms.[11] Transmissible modifications can spread in populations due to their impact on survival and reproduction, and they can become the basis for further modifications. Functionally organized traits, such as eyes or wings, are the result of this accumulation of selected modifications. *Ceteris paribus*, the more transmissible variation there is, the more a species can evolve via Darwinian selection dynamics.[12] Establishing the ubiquity of variation is crucial for demonstrating the significance of selection.[13] This explains why, after having written a "sketch" of his theory of evolution by means of selection in the early 1840s, Darwin decided to dedicate years of his life to the study of barnacles.[14]

The ubiquity of biological variation and what we have learned about useful ways of classifying such variation indicate that, for any species, there is no bundle of phenotypic traits present in its entirety in all and only the (actual and possible) members of the species. There are no phenotypic "characters"—to use Darwin's term—that are essential (necessary) for being human. Even if a phenotypic trait shared by all and only current humans could be identified, two humans could still produce offspring without the trait, and such offspring would still be considered human.[15]

There are phenotypic characters shared by many humans that are not present in other species, allowing for generalizations such as this: humans develop the ability to speak and understand natural languages. However, generalizations of this sort have exceptions: not all humans can speak and understand a natural language. Additionally, there are phenotypic traits shared by many humans and found also in other species, such as having four limbs. Yet, even in relation to traits like these, the species-level generalizations are not exceptionless: some humans do not have four limbs. Many important phenotypic traits are statistically typical in our species; identifying and describing these traits can be useful. However, these traits are not required for being human.

*

The idea of an essence as a bundle of necessary and sufficient conditions can be combined with the idea of an essence as an internal generative principle that causes and explains the observable manifestations of the essence itself. The ubiquity of phenotypic variation can coexist with a human essence understood as an internal generative cause if it can be shown that variation affects only the potentially unreliable manifestations of the internal generative principle and not the internal cause itself. From this perspective, the essence—the internal generative principle—remains invariant across the species, and it is in virtue of this that all humans are human. The invariant essence accounts for why various traits reliably appear and co-occur in humans, but the invariant essence does not manifest in the same way in each individual.

Nowadays, the internal generative principle is usually understood in terms of genes (or genetic structures, or gene regulatory networks). According to the genetic version of the invariant-bundle view, the human essence consists in a bundle of genetic (and genomic) traits. Each trait is individually necessary, and together they are jointly sufficient, for being human. On this view, the human essence is genetic (and genomic), not phenotypic; and there is overlap between the human essence and, say, the chimpanzee essence in so far as the essential genetic structures of the two species overlap.

Genetic structures are often said to *code for* phenotypes. This can be interpreted in two ways. On one interpretation, some specific genetic structures code for, say, limbs with certain features if those genetic structures (under statistically typical developmental circumstances) reliably and robustly cause the appearance of limbs with those features. On the other interpretation, some genetic structures code for limbs with certain features if those genetic structures were selectively favored due to their contribution (under circumstances that were typical when the selection occurred) to the development of limbs with those features. These are the "causal" and the "evolutionary" interpretations of the gene-encoding-phenotype language.[16] Both interpretations can be elaborated further, and their pros and cons debated. Importantly, on both interpretations, having a genetic trait that encodes a given phenotype does not guarantee that the organism will develop that phenotype. A genetically encoded trait might not be phenotypically manifested.[17]

Phenotypic development always requires multiple resources and is influenced—sometimes disruptively—by many different factors. Proponents of the view that the human essence is a bundle of genetic traits can argue that while the human genetic essence is invariant across the species, not all the phenotypic traits encoded in the genetic essence are phenotypically manifested in every member of the species. Every human has the human genetic essence but, in any given human, some phenotypic traits encoded by this essence might remain unexpressed. According to this perspective, the ubiquity of variation pertains to human phenotypes and to nonessential genetic structures; it does not pertain to the human genetic essence. If this view is adopted, one can develop a comprehensive account of human nature by identifying which genetic structures constitute the human genetic essence.

This way of thinking about human nature ought to be rejected. The ubiquity of variation affects both phenotypic and genetic traits.[18] New genetic variants appear very frequently, and some genetic modifications—specifically those in germ cells—can be passed down the generations. In general, there is no bundle of genetic structures present in its entirety in all and only the members of a species. Even if a genetic trait shared by all and only current humans could be identified, two humans can still produce offspring without the trait, and such offspring would still be human.

There are human genetic structures that are unique to our species. Some of these structures crucially contribute to the development of phenotypic traits that are distinctively human. For example, certain human-only genetic structures likely contribute to the development of our ability to speak and understand natural languages, even though not all humans develop this phenotypic trait and not all humans possess these specific genetic structures. Similarly, genetic structures that are present in both humans and some non-humans often account for phenotypic regularities that extend beyond the human species. For instance, there are genetic structures that explain why humans and other mammals typically have four limbs. However, not all humans have four limbs, and some humans do not have any limbs due to genetically rare traits, a condition known as *tetra-amelia syndrome*.

There is no need to invoke invariant genetic structures to explain the regularities observed in our species. There are no phenotypic traits that are essential (necessary) for being human, and there are no genetic traits that are essential (necessary) for being human.[19] Humans do not have an essence consisting of a species-invariant bundle of phenotypic traits, and they do not have an essence consisting of a species-invariant bundle of genetic traits.

Ideal Types and Genealogies

The chemical element uranium has an essence captured by the atomic number 92. This atomic number refers to the essential properties of the chemical element. Arguably, these essential properties constitute uranium's nature. If, due to the ubiquity of variation, no genetic or phenotypic traits can be said to be essential for being human, what could the human essence be? One possible answer is that the human essence, unlike the essence of chemical elements, must be understood in terms of an ideal type. According to the *ideal-type* version of the essentialist concept, the human essence—and thus human nature—is a bundle of traits that is present not in all humans but only in ideal-type humans. The properties in this bundle are essential (necessary) for being *fully* human, for being an ideal-type human; they are not essential for simply being human. Individuals who lack some properties in the bundle can still be considered human—if, say, they have enough of those properties—but these individuals are less than fully human. They are not ideal-type humans; they do not partake fully in the human essence. Every atom of uranium is fully uranium, but not every human is fully human.[20]

Ideal-type essentialism is compatible with the claim that all properties in the essential bundle are phenotypic (manifested) traits, but it can also be combined with the idea that the properties in the essential bundle are genetic. Moreover, ideal-type essentialism can be combined with different views about the actual existence of ideal-type humans. It is compatible for example with the view that the ideal-type human is a Platonic blueprint that can only be imperfectly instantiated in actual, mundane beings; it is also compatible with the view that ideal-type humans existed in the past or will exist in the future, but do not exist in the present. The simplest and possibly most common ideal-type view is that some current humans are fully human, in that they fully partake in the human essence, while others are not. Aristotle seems to endorse an account of this sort, and many folk accounts appear to have a similar structure.

Ideal-type essentialism allows for classifying humans in relation to how closely they resemble the ideal type. It makes it possible to claim that some categories of humans are farther from the ideal type than others. Hence, it makes it possible to claim that some categories of humans are less fully human than others. The farther from the ideal type you are, the less fully human you are.

One issue for ideal-type essentialism is this: from a Darwinian biological perspective, there are no ideal-type species members or ideal-type traits. There are variants that are widespread in the species and variants that are rare, variants that reoccur cross-generationally and variants that do not, variants that are closer to the species average and variants that are farther away from it, variants that are developmentally robust and variants that are not, variants that are favored by selection and variants that are not, and so on. Biologically speaking, all variants are, at least potentially, interesting and worth taking note of. It is by measuring and analyzing genetic and phenotypic variation that evolutionary theory, broadly conceived, allows us to generate explanations of how species change over time and, thereby, explanations of complex traits. Variation is not an epiphenomenon. The study of variation is one of the main tools of Darwinian evolutionary theory.[21]

A tempting thought is that Darwinian selection might allow us to identify a privileged bundle of traits. The traits essential for being fully human, for being an ideal-type human, would be those favored by selection. However, Darwinian selection is always context-dependent and contingent. Some variants may be favored by selection at one moment in time, but circumstances—and selection pressures—might change. Variants that were once advantageous might become disadvantageous, and vice versa. For example, new pathogens might suddenly appear and render disadvantageous social interactions (say, kissing or handshaking) that were once advantageous. A resource that was common (say, a particular kind of prey) might suddenly disappear as a result of climate change or over-hunting, transforming once advantageous skills into burdens.[22]

Human evolution, just like the evolution of any other species, has been affected by contingent changes in selection pressures. There is no way to pick out a bundle of to-be-selected "characters" independent of the context, and there is no biologically privileged context. If human evolution inevitably tended toward a single and predetermined outcome, an evolutionarily privileged state, the ideal type could perhaps be identified with that final outcome, irrespective of the vagaries of the selection processes. Those who are closer to that final outcome would be "more evolved" and thereby more fully human than those who are farther from it. But human evolution is not a progression toward a prefixed end.

Questions about the existence and features of an ideal type for humans are best seen as questions about how humans ought to be. An ideal type is an evaluative standard. General questions about the way humans ought to be cannot be settled with reference to biological criteria alone once a teleological account of biological species has been abandoned. Biologically speaking, there is no way in which humans ought to be. Biologically speaking, humans do not have a purpose, or a function, or a destiny. Through various conceptual and nonconceptual strategies, the idea that humans have a *telos* has been removed from biological theorizing.[23] What humans ought to be depends on whether there are normatively authoritative evaluative standards that apply to humans, and on what these standards are. These standards (if they exist) cannot be derived solely from biological findings and cannot be identified solely through biological theorizing.[24]

*

We can use the term "bio-essentialist" to refer to accounts according to which human nature is an essence that can be characterized purely in biological terms. The invariant-bundle bio-essentialist account does not work, nor does the bio-essentialist version of the ideal-type account. Is there any other bio-essentialist view worth exploring? In contemporary biological theorizing, it is common to argue that a human organism is human not in virtue of its genetic structures or phenotypic traits, but rather in virtue of the way it is genealogically connected to other organisms. Genealogy, in this context, refers to biological reproduction and to ancestor-descendant lineages. The *tree of life* is not the biblical tree of eternal life, but rather the totality of biological lineages, comprising all ancestor-descendant relationships connecting living beings on Planet Earth.

The idea that life on our planet can be conceived of as a tree linking all biological organisms plays a central role in Darwin's explanatory narratives. We are all "netted together," he says.[25] Closely linked to this idea is the view that "classification [in biology] consists in grouping beings according to their actual *relationship*, i.e. their consanguinity, or descent from common stocks" and that "all true classification is genealogical; that community of descent is the hidden bond which naturalists have been unconsciously seeking."[26] One way to put it is this: an organism belongs to a given species if and only if it is a part of—it is reproductively embedded in—a given section of the genealogical tree of life. If one is looking for biological properties that all and only humans have, relational properties of this sort can do the trick. Being reproductively embedded in a given section of the tree of life can be said to be both necessary and sufficient for an organism to be human; one can define the human essence in bio-genealogical terms.[27] This is a nonintuitive way of thinking about the human essence; intuitive everyday essentialism conceives of essences in terms of intrinsic properties, not in terms of relations between the organism and something extrinsic or external to it.[28] Nonetheless, one can stretch the intuitive notion of essence to make room for relational essences.

Could human nature be a bio-genealogical relational essence of this sort? A view that equates human nature with species membership bio-genealogically defined does not align well with an attempt to take seriously the links between human praxis and ideas about human nature. Let us consider invariant-bundle bio-essentialist views. These ways of thinking about human nature, if they worked, could provide a decent communication channel between, on the one hand, scientifically well-supported ideas about what we fundamentally are and, on the other, conversations and decisions about human futures. Scientific discoveries about the genotypic or phenotypic constituents of the invariant bundle could inform our conversations and decisions about our modes of life. Similarly, a bio-essentialist ideal-type view could, in a way, provide a decent channel, as biology could tell us how humans ought to be and thereby guide our praxis-oriented reflections about which modes of life to conserve, change, pursue, or avoid. However, accepting a view that identifies human nature with a bio-genealogical essence would mean accepting a way of thinking about human nature that cannot properly function as a communication channel in the relevant sense.

A useful concept of human nature needs more content than a bio-genealogical account can provide. The fact that all and only humans belong to a particular section of the bio-genealogical tree of life is important and interesting. This fact can be used definitionally and taxonomically. But this fact alone is of limited use in the context of reflections about our modes of life and what, if anything, could or should be done about them. Facts about our non-invariant "corporeal and mental endowments" are often highly relevant and informative in conversations and decisions about our modes of life, even though they cannot be used definitionally.[29] The issue of what we fundamentally are (as as opposed, perhaps, to the issue of who is included in the "we") cannot plausibly be resolved in purely bio-genealogical terms.[30]

*

If bio-essentialist accounts fail, it might be worth checking whether any nonbiological version of essentialism could work. One possible (and traditional) view is this: having an immaterial supernatural soul with certain characteristics is both necessary and sufficient for being human; the human essence is the human soul and variation in nonsupernatural (corporeal) traits is irrelevant. Different versions of this view attribute different features to human souls and provide varied explanations of the links between such souls and bodies. On an essentialist account like this, discovering what we fundamentally are involves learning about our supernatural souls, which, in turn, can help us determine what we ought to do about our modes of life. Obviously, in response to the immaterial-soul way of thinking about the human essence, one can draw attention to the best available arguments against the belief in immaterial souls.[31]

A different nonbiological version of essentialism involves the attempt to characterize the human essence in purely evaluative terms. Let us revisit the idea that the human essence is the bundle of properties required for being fully human, and that being fully human means being the way humans ought to be. Twenty-first-century biologists cannot, *qua* biologists, tell us how humans ought to be, but this is compatible with the view that there are evaluative standards that determine what it takes to be fully human. Such standards can be identified not through biological theory but through evaluative reflection. Once the relevant standards are identified, we might discover, for instance, that certain forms of practical rationality are essential for being fully human and living a fully human life. On a view like this, evaluative criteria determine the kind of human essence (or at least one kind of human essence) that we may need to invoke in discussions and decisions about human futures.[32]

This proposal can be developed in many ways, but, for current purposes, we can focus on one single and general issue. If referring to human essential traits is merely a way of saying how humans ought to be according to the evaluative standards one deems appropriate, then it is better to drop the essence talk and make one's preferred evaluative standards explicit, along with any arguments for such standards. Putting the label "essential" on the traits that one prefers adds no genuine argumentative force to the relevant evaluative claims. It does add some rhetorical force, since it chimes with intuitively powerful essentialist tendencies and biases. However, at least in general, dressing up disagreements about evaluative matters with essentialist clothes is undesirable, for it can make such disagreements less transparent than they need to be.

Debates about human nature have an impact on human praxis. The communication channel between ideas about what we fundamentally are and conversations or decisions about our modes of life is, in some respects, a two-way channel. But if this channel is allowed to collapse in on itself, much is lost in terms of our ability to "rationally regulate" human praxis. This can occur whenever debates about human nature are allowed to become *immediately and directly* debates about how humans ought to be, and vice versa.[33]

After Essentialism

It has been suggested that human nature, if understood in essentialist terms, is a "superstition."[34] If this is right, and human nature is not an essence, should we try to elaborate a respectable non-essentialist alternative to the essentialist concept? Or should we become eliminativists about human nature?[35] Ideas about human nature will, most likely, continue to play a role in conversations and decisions about human futures. Understanding the concept of human nature as a channel connecting ideas about what we fundamentally are and human praxis can motivate us to avoid eliminativist approaches. If a suitable alternative to the essentialist concept can be constructed, it will be possible for those wishing to overcome their essentialist intuitions to do so.

Compare the essentialist ways of thinking about human nature with, for example, the prescientific folk-physical ways of thinking about simultaneity. In the folk-physical view, if two events are simultaneous, they are so in an absolute way, regardless of any frame of reference. However, scientific physics tells us that this is wrong. According to Einstein's theory of relativity, the simultaneity of two events is only relative to a specific inertial frame, and there is no privileged frame of reference. The same events that occur simultaneously in one inertial frame are not simultaneous in another inertial frame. Scientifically speaking, there is no such thing as absolute simultaneity. Absolute simultaneity is a "superstition."

Considering that the folk-physical view of simultaneity is inadequate, one could, in principle, make an eliminativist proposal and argue that, since there is no such thing as absolute simultaneity, we should abandon simultaneity talk. However, retaining the same term for (nonexistent) absolute simultaneity and (really real) relative simultaneity allows those wishing to overcome their absolutist folk-physical intuitions to easily identify a way to do so. Constructing an alternative to the absolutist concept of simultaneity is better than being eliminativist about simultaneity. Although there are important differences between the two cases, one could argue that constructing an alternative to the essentialist concept of human nature is similarly better than being eliminativist about human nature.

The relativistic alternative to the absolutist way of thinking about simultaneity plays a role in specialized contexts that are handled by experts. The relativistic concept of simultaneity is used in GPS calculations to achieve accuracy. Nonexperts do not need to use the post-absolutist concept in their daily pursuits. In contrast, a post-essentialist concept of human nature could be employed in conversations and decisions about human futures, and could be embraced (at least in principle) by anyone able and willing to join those conversations and make those decisions. Any suitable post-essentialist concept of human nature would need to align with the Darwinian evolutionary framework, incorporating what we know about the ubiquity of variation, and with other portions of empirical science for which there is strong evidential support. It would, moreover, need to function adequately in relation to our conversations and decisions about human futures, including those that occur outside of scientific communities.[36]

5

Post-Essentialism

Statistical Typicality

According to what can be called the *statistical-typicality concept* of human nature, a trait is part of human nature only if it is statistically typical in current humans. Various attempts to find an alternative to the essentialist concept adopt one version or another of the statistical-typicality concept.[1]

Statistical typicality is not ideal typicality. The statistically typical need not match any ideal type and the instances of an ideal type can be statistically rare or even nonexistent. Moreover, statistical typicality is a vague notion. How frequent does a variant need to be in order to be statistically typical? There is no non-arbitrary cut-off point, but for practical purposes it can be stipulated that a variant is statistically (species) typical if it is present, say, in at least 90 percent of extant species members. Another consideration has to do with how organisms change as they progress in their life cycle. For example, most human children do not babble at birth, but they start babbling within the first few months of life; the babbling starts fading during the second year of life, as recognizable words take its place. Therefore, babbling itself is not statistically typical in humans, but babbling during the first few years of life is statistically typical in our species.

Nowadays, as a result of globalization and multinational corporations, there are brand names and logos that are instantly recognized by the vast majority of humans. Does recognition of these brands and logos constitute part of human nature? If you want to exclude phenotypic traits like these from human nature, as advocates of the statistical-typicality view generally do, you could argue that statistical typicality alone is necessary but not sufficient to classify something as part of human nature. But what other criteria might be required in addition to statistical typicality?

One suggestion is that any component of human nature must be both statistically typical and unaffected by environmental factors. However, it is important to recognize that development always involves environmental factors. Genes by themselves do not do anything.[2] It is easy to overlook the importance of the environment. The gravitational pull on the surface of our planet (approximately 9.8 m/s^2) is not usually considered a factor in human musculoskeletal development. But if you start thinking about how human bones and muscles would develop under a different gravitational pull (e.g., on Mars, with its gravitational pull of 3.7 m/s^2), you soon realize the importance of this factor.[3]

A related suggestion is that any component of human nature must not only be statistically typical but also inborn. However, babbling tendencies are not present at birth; yet many argue that they are part of human nature. Given cases like this, one could drop the idea that the relevant traits must be inborn and claim instead that statistically typical traits are part of human nature only if they develop reliably and robustly, in regular and predictable ways. But, many traits whose development requires learning are developmentally reliable and robust in the relevant sense.

Consider these human-specific abilities: the ability to imitate (and learn through imitation), the ability to ascribe thoughts and feelings to others (mindreading), and the ability to identify and follow social norms (normative thinking). Cecilia Heyes argues that these traits are "cognitive gadgets" rather than "cognitive instincts." Cognitive instincts are cognitive traits that do not require learning for their development, whereas cognitive gadgets are assembled through learning.[4] According to Heyes (and contrary to the mainstream opinion in cognitive psychology), imitation, mindreading, and normative thinking develop through various forms of socially scaffolded learning processes. On her view, these traits, in their statistically typical forms, develop reliably and predictably due to structured interactions between learning mechanisms and learning environments.[5]

Let us also consider the belief that water is wet, a human phenotypic trait that is statistically typical. This belief is acquired through perception and cognition, and it is generally acquired by all humans except for those who die early in life or experience severe perceptual and cognitive impairments. The presence of robust and reliably predictable developmental patterns does not negate the involvement of learning.[6]

According to another suggestion, any component of human nature needs to be statistically typical and, in addition, it needs to have an evolutionary history, in the sense that the trait needs to be the outcome of Darwinian genetic selection or, more generally, of frequency changes in the human gene pool.[7] However, learned traits can, and often do, have an evolutionary history in this sense. Let us imagine an ancestral population where some individuals can easily acquire a valuable skill through learning, while others cannot. We can suppose that the difference between those who acquire the skill and those who do not is due, in part, to genetic differences: only individuals with certain genetic elements can learn the valuable skill. If the skill is advantageous in terms of survival and reproduction, Darwinian selection can favor those genetic elements, leading to their increased frequency and to a greater proportion of the population acquiring the skill. In this way, a learned skill that is initially rare can become statistically typical. The genetic evolution of traits involving learning is a complex topic, but it is clear that a "genetically evolved" trait can be one that, for its development, requires learning in addition to specific genetic resources.[8] Appealing to the distinction between traits that are genetically evolved and traits that are not cannot help those who want to exclude learned traits from human nature.[9]

As mentioned earlier, there are ways of making sense of the idea that genetic structures code for phenotypic traits. If you like to think in terms of genetic encoding, you might want to consider the claim that the additional requirement for inclusion in human nature (alongside statistical typicality) is genetic encoding. On this view, only traits that are both statistically typical and genetically encoded should be seen as part of human nature. However, if genetic encoding is understood in terms of developmental reliability, traits whose development requires learning can count as genetically encoded; and the same holds if genetic encoding is understood in terms of genetic selection.

Some statistical-typicality accounts suggest that the additional ingredient is explanatory significance: only statistically typical traits that are explanatorily significant can be said to be part of human nature.[10] This suggestion aligns well with the idea that ways of thinking about human nature are ways of thinking about (some aspects of) what we fundamentally are. However, even with a view like this, there is still room for learned traits to be classified as part of human nature. Imitation, mindreading, and normative thinking are explanatorily significant: we cannot explain human behavior and societies without mentioning them. This remains true even if it turns out that these traits, as Heyes argues, are the product of interactions between statistically typical learning mechanisms and socially scaffolded learning environments.

Should traits whose development involves learning be excluded from human nature? Before saying more on this issue, some matters concerning human variation require clarification. We need to consider the general implications of making statistical typicality a necessary requirement for being part of human nature.[11]

Human Diversity

Darwinian selection can result in organisms developing different traits in response to different circumstances. A simple instance of adaptive plasticity can be observed in the moths of the species *Biston robustum*. When these organisms are caterpillars, they resemble the twigs of the trees they are born on, typically camellia, chinquapin, or cherry trees. This resemblance provides protection against predators. If a caterpillar born on a camellia is fed cherry leaves, it will eventually resemble the twigs of a cherry tree, and vice versa. The caterpillars share genetic and physiological traits that give rise to distinct morphological traits in response to differences in diet. This is the result of a selection process that favors individuals capable of using dietary cues for camouflage.[12]

Another instance of adaptive plasticity is the sex switching (sequential hermaphroditism) found in many coral reef fish. There are species where protandry (a male to female switch) occurs, species where protogyny (a female to male switch) occurs, and species with bidirectional change. A female might switch to male upon reaching a certain size, while a male might switch to female if there are bigger males around. The switching mechanisms respond to changes in environmental and social circumstances.[13]

Perceptual and cognitive mechanisms are mechanisms of adaptive plasticity. In humans, the belief that water is wet is the outcome of adaptively plastic mechanisms, even if acquiring this belief is virtually inevitable in standard circumstances, which routinely involve encounters with water in liquid form. The perceptual and cognitive mechanisms that produce this belief also produce many other mental states, including many that vary across the species. Heyes proposes that forms of associative learning play a role in the development of statistically typical human traits such as imitation, mindreading, and normative thinking. The very same learning mechanisms also contribute to human psychological and behavioral variation. Undoubtedly, various types of learning mechanisms and niche-constructed learning environments are responsible for the phenomenon Rousseau sought to capture with the term "perfectibility."

The immune system is another significant source of adaptive plasticity. It has been selected to generate different responses in different circumstances (mainly attacks from pathogens). In novel circumstances, the immune system can produce novel responses. The response can be beneficial, such as the identification and elimination of a new pathogen, but occasionally it can be harmful, as in the case of an environmentally triggered autoimmune disease. Adaptively plastic mechanisms can produce new traits, which can be good or bad for the individual and can, in some cases, become statistically typical.[14]

Phenotypic variation resulting from adaptive plasticity is not the only kind of variation that can be explained via Darwinian dynamics. In some cases, selection favors one single variant, and this favored variant might invade the whole species and become statistically typical. In other cases, two or more alternative variants might be favored and no single variant become statistically typical. This can happen, for example, when different parts of the physical or social niche make different traits advantageous.[15]

Lactase is the enzyme responsible for lactose digestion; lactose is a sugar present in high quantities in fresh (unfermented) milk. The ability to digest lactose-rich food in childhood is statistically typical in current humans. Some humans retain this ability as adults, a phenomenon known as lactase persistence. Lactase persistence is observed predominantly in individuals whose ancestors relied on unfermented milk from domesticated animals as a significant source of nutrients. In these specific populations, strong selection pressures favored the persistence of lactase production into adulthood. In contrast, populations that did not heavily depend on unfermented milk as a dietary source experienced different selection pressures.[16] Lactase persistence was selectively favored in some populations but not in others.

Likewise, differences in the abundance of sunlight affected the evolution of skin pigmentation in our species. Sunlight exposure is crucial for human health as it enables vitamin D synthesis. But excessive sunlight exposure can be harmful, as it can result in cancer or other health problems. Lighter skin facilitates vitamin D synthesis, while darker skin provides more photoprotection. Therefore, darker skin was an advantage in populations living in sunlight-rich areas, and lighter skin was an advantage in sunlight-poor areas.[17]

As for behavioral strategies, being favored by selection can depend on the strategies that other conspecifics are likely to adopt, the frequencies of alternative strategies, and the structure of interactions.[18] Strategies for finding a reproductive partner, even if successful when competitors use different strategies, might become inefficient when too many competitors adopt the same strategy.[19] Specific ways of being cooperative might be advantageous when interacting with conspecifics with matching cooperative strategies, but disadvantageous when encountering uncooperative or exploitative individuals.

For obvious reasons, human behavioral and psychological differences—in personality traits, sexual preferences, aggressiveness, educational attainment, financial success, and so on—are an important focus of attention, but we still have limited knowledge about the observed patterns of variation. When phenotypic differences are partly associated with genetic differences, as indicated, for example, by twin studies or by genome-wide association studies, we often do not know whether the genetic variation exists because of selection dynamics or because of nonselective processes. In general, the causal links between genetic variation and measurable phenotypic outcomes are complex and involve (directly and indirectly) multiple environmental and social factors. Changes in environmental and social factors often alter the ways in which genetic variation is reflected in phenotypic variation. This also means that phenotypic differences resulting from genetic differences can be shaped through environmental and social (nongenetic) means. In many cases, this may well be the best way to proceed. The more we learn about these intricate mappings, the better we become at intervening in ways that are likely to produce desired results.[20]

We have evolved powerful ways of modifying ourselves that are not present in other species. We can modify ourselves through collective learning and cumulative cultural dynamics. We can modify ourselves through praxis driven by political, moral, or aesthetic goals and criteria. Through science, we can acquire sophisticated technological tools of transformation. These tools constitute new forms of social mediation between genotypes and phenotypes, and between phenotypes and phenotypes. This process can generate new differences and eliminate old ones, and it both affects and is affected by the web of social conflicts.[21]

*

Let us look briefly at sex differences and let us consider the broader biological context. In humans and many other sexually reproducing animal species, there are two types of gametes (anisogamy) and most individuals have either ova-producing gonads (gonadal femaleness) or sperm-producing gonads (gonadal maleness). In some anisogamous species, such as earthworms and barnacles, individuals generally have both ova-producing and sperm-producing gonadal tissue (simultaneous hermaphroditism). In non-hermaphroditic (gonochoric) species, the presence in a single individual of the two types of gonadal tissue is rare, although not impossible. A small percentage of humans have both male and female gonadal tissue, a condition known as *ovotesticular syndrome*.[22]

Gonadal females and gonadal males often face different types of selection pressures. This is due to the differences between ova production and sperm production, but also to the morphological, physiological, and behavioral traits that become associated with the two types of gonads. In many species, gonadal females and gonadal males also have different genital organs. As always, there are exceptions: some gonadal males may develop genitals that are typically found in gonadally female conspecifics, and vice versa, and there can be cases where a mix of male and female genitals is found. Female and male genitals face different selective pressures: for example, certain infections or types of cancer can affect female reproductive organs more than male reproductive organs, and vice versa.[23] The same applies to other traits. For example, in a species where usually only individuals with male gonads and genitals develop horns, the males are exposed to horn-related selection pressures to which the females are not directly exposed.

In a small number of mammal species, including the platypus, gonadal females lay eggs. In all other mammals, gonadal females incubate the fertilized ova and internally gestate their offspring before giving birth.[24] Gonadally female mammals are also able to lactate and nurse their young after birth (platypuses included, although they lack nipples). Pregnancy, birthing, and nursing generate selection pressures on gonadally female mammals that do not directly affect the males. However, there can be indirect effects. Nipples, in those mammals that have them, serve as an example. Male nipples are a result of lactation-related selection pressures that affect females directly but have indirect effects on males' bodies. Some have suggested that, in humans and other primates, "female orgasms" are a by-product of selection for ejaculation-inducing "male orgasms." However, this hypothesis is unsupported. Given the numerous functions of sex and sexual pleasure, there could plausibly have been selection for orgasms across the gonadal and genital divides.[25]

The extent to which gonadal females and gonadal males take care of their young after birth varies significantly across species. In species with offspring care, gonadal females often invest more than gonadal males in the care of the young, but there are also many species where gonadal males invest more than gonadal females.[26] One possible outcome of the selection for offspring care is the development of psychological dispositions that make it pleasurable for adult individuals to interact with and provide assistance to young conspecifics. In humans, care of the young tends to be highly cooperative, and more so than in many other primates. Cooperative childcare tendencies in humans are likely the result of the ways in which female strategies and alliances shaped the selection pressures acting on our ancestors.[27]

In mammals, genetic factors trigger the developmental pathways leading organisms to their gonadal and then genital sex. However, many reptile, amphibian, and fish species exhibit environmental sex determination. As we saw, in some of these species, an environmentally induced switch from one gonadal/genital sex to another can be observed. There are also species, such as some reptiles, that combine environmental and genetic sex determination. In species with genetic sex determination, one of the most common systems is the XX/XY system. This is also the system present in humans. XY at a chromosomal level generally leads to gonadal/genital maleness, while XX leads to gonadal/genital femaleness. It is important to note that the development of gonadal and genital traits involves many genetic factors shared across the sexes, and that there are XY humans who are not gonadally or genitally male, XX humans who are not gonadally or genitally female, and humans who are neither XX nor XY.

When studying human sex-related differences, one realizes that there are many layers to consider, from the molecular to the social. In some of these layers, the relevant differences are quasi-discrete. This is what happens in the chromosomal, gonadal, and genital layers; the "quasi" is needed to stress that, even within these layers, there are individuals who are *intersex* and do not fit into the relevant binaries. In other layers, one can often observe a continuum between two poles. In many cases, the average differences between "males" and "females" are small and the overlap in the range of variation is significant. Sperm-making humans are, on average, taller than ova-making humans, but many ova-making humans are taller than many sperm-making humans.[28]

Complexity exists in the links between the chromosomal, gonadal, and genital layers; and the complexity increases when one focuses on the other layers, including the psychological and social ones.[29] Culturally variable gender roles and discourses, with their performative effects, have an impact on sex-associated human differences. This applies particularly to behavioral and psychological differences, but not exclusively. When social circumstances change, many behavioral or psychological differences associated with chromosomal, gonadal, or genital sex change too, and in various cases, they disappear or are reversed.[30] We still know too little about these processes and about how sex-related differences could be transformed by yet-to-come social circumstances. But we know that the niche-constructed environment is important. This knowledge stems from the numerous phenotypic changes brought about in the last few centuries by human praxis. These changes include those due to techno-scientific praxis, but also those brought about by the activities of feminist and gender-diverse thinkers and movements. Whether or not you like these transformations, and whether or not you would like to see further transformations, these changes are significant.

It is important to emphasize that what we know about the different layers and interactions tells us that distinguishing between sex-related differences that are purely biological and sex-related differences that are purely social is misleading. Gender roles and other social factors directly and indirectly affect many molecular and developmental processes; and gender norms are partly shaped by entrenched dynamics where genes, gonads, and genitals play various (indirect and mediated) roles.[31]

*

Other kinds of human differences worth considering are disabilities and mental disorders. Many conditions classified as disabilities have a genetic basis, but we often do not know why the relevant variants are present in the gene pool.[32] In many cases, we also do not know much about the processes linking the genetic traits to the relevant conditions. A case where we do know something is phenylketonuria (PKU), a genetic condition that, through an atypical metabolic process, leads to neurological problems and intellectual disability. It has been discovered that, through dietary changes, the metabolic problem could in principle be circumvented, thus preventing the occurrence of neurological problems. Diets mediate between genetic structures and phenotypic outcomes.

In studies on the etiology of conditions classified as mental disorders, researchers often seek to uncover how social factors mediate the emergence of these conditions. Schizophrenia and psychosis are commonly believed to result from the interaction between an individual's genome and circumstances such as poverty, abuse, or trauma. Social structures and systems influence the impact of conditions classified as disabilities or mental disorders on individuals' lives. The details vary from condition to condition. Transport infrastructures affect the lives of individuals without limbs differently from the way they affect the lives of individuals with cystic fibrosis. Capitalist job markets have a different impact on individuals with Asperger syndrome and individuals with Down syndrome. One kind of social mediation that is important is the social stigma that negatively affects those classified as disabled or mentally ill. Social labels matter. This can motivate attempts to introduce new labels, new classifications, and new ways of thinking about these traits.

*

Gonadal maleness and traits associated with it are not statistically typical in our species as a whole; the same applies to gonadal femaleness and associated traits. Nevertheless, the existence of multiple layers of sex differences, linked in complex ways, is significant. Many conditions ordinarily classified as disabilities and mental disorders are statistically atypical but not uncommon. Corporeal and mental "divergence" from the statistical norm plays an important role in many different social contexts. Variation in skin pigmentation has been affected by selection pressures for photoprotection and for enabling vitamin D synthesis. In the last 500 years, through complex historical processes unrelated to photoprotection and vitamin D synthesis, differences in skin pigmentation have become associated with various kinds of social inequalities in various countries. Racialization and related phenomena have transformed the impact and significance of variation in skin color.

Not all the dimensions of human variation are equally interesting; and different dimensions of human variation can be interesting in different ways. One thing to notice is that if a pattern of variation in genetic or phenotypic traits turns out to be important in scientific theorizing, this pattern is likely to become salient in at least some conversations and decisions about human futures. Likewise, if a pattern of variation turns out to be important in some conversations about human futures, scientific experts are likely to take a theoretical and empirical interest in it due to economic and reputational incentives.

Making statistical typicality a necessary condition for being part of human nature creates a disconnect between accounts of important patterns of human variation and the language of human nature. Given the impact that ideas about human nature have on human praxis, this is undesirable. Such disconnect, among other consequences, can lead to the marginalization or disregard of some human groups (characterized by variants that are not species-typical) in conversations and decisions about human futures, including conversations and decisions that steer the direction of future scientific research. A concept of human nature that makes room for important dimensions of variation can help us avoid this.

Proponents of the statistical-typicality view may agree that good scientific research and good conversations about human futures need to pay attention to important patterns of variation. But they may also insist that these patterns need not be included in our descriptions of human nature, which should focus exclusively on (some theoretically interesting subset of) statistically typical traits. However, this way of defending the statistical-typicality concept does not properly come to terms with how our thoughts and actions are affected by ideas about human nature. In a variety of important contexts, many humans tend to think in terms of essences and ideal types, and to conflate what is statistically abnormal with what is evaluatively abnormal, substandard, and inferior. These tendencies are due to a variety of entrenched psychological and social factors. Making room for dimensions of variation and atypical traits within our concept of human nature is a way of counteracting these tendencies, thereby potentially improving the quality of our conversations and decisions.[33]

A good non-essentialist concept of human nature should allow us to see important human differences (genetic and phenotypic) as part of a diverse human nature. The human is plural.[34] Among the important patterns, there are both patterns of genetic and phenotypic similarity (including patterns of species-typicality) and patterns of genetic and phenotypic difference. An account of human nature that fails to mention these important patterns is, arguably, an incomplete account.[35]

Human Niches and Human Praxis

Learning is the most abundant source of adaptive plasticity, but this is compatible with the view that traits whose development involves learning can be part of human nature, if they are sufficiently important. Heyes argues that imitation, mindreading, and normative thinking require, for their reliable development, specific interactions between social learning mechanisms and socially inherited social niches. Whether or not she is right, it is undoubtedly the case that without imitation, mindreading, and normative thinking, our modes of life would be very different from what they currently are. Without these traits, human praxis would resemble what can be observed in non-human primates. Imitation, mindreading, and normative thinking explain many features that humans individually and collectively possess. Arguably, an account of human nature that fails to mention these traits is an incomplete account.[36]

What we are now is, in some fundamental respects, different from what our ancestors were before these traits became species-typical. It should be said, however, that a significant minority of humans are "neurodivergent" with respect to species-typical mindreading skills. This is an important fact about humans, both from a scientific perspective and from a general praxis-oriented standpoint.[37] Similar claims could arguably be made for imitation and normative thinking. When describing human nature, we should mention not only statistically typical mindreading, imitation, and normative thinking, but also the relevant patterns of divergence.

*

WEIRD stands for Western, Educated, Industrialized, Rich, Democratic. Joseph Henrich argues that many psychological traits widespread in WEIRD societies are relatively uncommon elsewhere.

On his account, WEIRD individuals are more individualistic, self-centered, and more willing to engage in impersonal forms of cooperation, including those relying on market mechanisms.[38] Non-WEIRD individuals, in contrast, prioritize personal connections and prefer forms of cooperation that rely on kin structures and long-term alliances. According to Henrich, many WEIRD traits are often considered species-typical simply because, for many decades, influential research has been conducted primarily on WEIRD research participants, by WEIRD researchers, in WEIRD countries and institutions. But cross-cultural research shows that WEIRDness is not statistically typical.

In Henrich's narrative, all human societies were once non-WEIRD. Over the last 1,000 years or so, some societies have become increasingly WEIRD. The original trigger for this shift was a contingent historical event: the family and marriage policies of the Catholic Church. Those policies led to the erosion of kin-based networks and institutions, and to the emergence of more impersonal social systems.[39] Henrich suggests that the rise of WEIRDness has been a cumulative cultural process, involving causal loops whereby new social practices (such as those promoted by religious authorities) favored the selective retention and spread of WEIRD psychological tendencies. These tendencies, in turn, resulted in WEIRDer social practices, which led to WEIRDer tendencies. And so on.

In Western Europe, according to this account, the gradual breaking up of kin-based networks and an increased reliance on market mechanisms promoted social and technological innovation. This allowed some European societies to aggressively extend their sphere of economic, military, cultural, and political influence, resulting in Western capitalism (and colonialism). The rise of WEIRD societies exerted pressure on other societies, some of which started adopting WEIRD modes of life and adapting them to their local circumstances. Henrich believes that the cultural emergence and spread of WEIRD traits and institutions can help explain current global inequalities.

The account can be criticized on various grounds. It may in the end turn out that the WEIRD/non-WEIRD pattern is in some ways illusory, or that it is not explanatorily significant, or that it is real and significant but not in the ways suggested by Henrich. But I would like to discuss the account's general structure rather than its details.[40] The account illustrates the interconnection of human praxis, learning abilities, psychological variation, and variation in socially inherited social niches. Human actions can result in the appearance and spread of new psychological variants. The kind of learning abilities that are common in our species, which make complex cultural constructions possible, produce variation. However, a focus on statistically typical cultural learning does not provide much information on cultural constructions and their local or global effects. Many human psychological traits can only be identified and understood by studying the cumulative cultural processes that have generated them. As Henrich, Muthukrishna, and Slingerland put it:

> Psychology needs to become a historical science if it wants to be a genuinely universal science of human cognition and behavior.[41]

An account of human psychology that fails to mention important dimensions of cultural variation is incomplete. A good concept of human nature should work as a communication channel between what we are learning about important patterns of similarity and difference in human "characters," including patterns that turn out to be culturally caused, and conversations on to-be-pursued and to-be-avoided human futures. Important patterns of culturally caused phenotypic variation, just like other important patterns of phenotypic variation, should be included in our descriptions of human nature.

*

Socially constructed niches affect the selection pressures acting on genetic and phenotypic variants. One example of this is the coevolution of food-processing techniques and what are now species-typical features of our digestive systems. Compared to other primates, we have small mouths and teeth, weak muscles in lips and jaws, small stomachs, and short colons. We are also not very efficient at detoxifying wild foods. These human characters are due to the ways our social niches have been influenced by culturally transmitted food-processing techniques, such as "cooking, drying, pounding, grinding, leaching, chopping, marinating, smoking, and scraping."[42] These techniques have resulted in an externalization of some parts of our digestive processes and, thereby, in a reduction of the internal digestive workload. The presence of these techniques selected for genes that reliably build smaller mouths, smaller stomachs, and so on. The reduction of the internal digestive workload contributed, moreover, to genetic selection processes that resulted in larger brains. If fewer metabolic resources need to be used in the construction and operation of the digestive system, more resources can be used to build and utilize brains. If less time needs to be spent, say, chewing food, more time can be spent performing more stimulating tasks.[43]

In his 1978 book on human nature, E.O. Wilson wrote that "genes hold culture on a leash."[44] In the last few decades, gene-culture coevolutionary theorists have instead shown that cultural processes often determine the direction of travel of human genetic evolution.[45] Human praxis and socially inherited niches are the primary drivers of human genetic evolution.

Human praxis and inherited niches are responsible for the genetic evolution of some human species-typical traits but also for evolved patterns of genetic variation where no variant is species-typical. In some human populations, genes for lactase persistence are present in part due to the ancestry of these populations, which can be traced back to groups that had the cultural knowledge and skills to domesticate animals and extract milk from them. Similarly, some populations have genes that result in lighter skin pigmentation partly because they are descendants of groups that left areas with abundant sunlight and moved to—and were able to culturally adapt to—areas with less abundant sunlight. By moving to new areas, those ancestral groups passed down new environments to their descendants, and thereby also new genetic selection pressures. Moving to a new area, a form of niche selection, is itself a form of niche construction.

*

Contemporary humans have brains and bodies that allow them (in general and in given circumstances) to interact with others in relatively peaceful and productive ways. How did we get these (imperfect) cooperation-conducive traits? One hypothesis worth exploring is that, in our lineage, there has been genetic selection against certain forms of violence and for "corporeal and mental endowments" that make those forms of violence less likely to occur. An additional hypothesis is that this selective process has been driven by political desires and collective praxis.

According to Christopher Boehm, the small-scale hunter-gatherer societies that are most representative of the modes of life of our Late Pleistocene ancestors exhibit *reverse dominance hierarchies*.[46] In other great apes, such as chimpanzees and gorillas, alpha males dominate the whole group primarily through violence and the threat of violence.[47] In contrast, violent would-be alphas are routinely neutralized by the rank and file in hunter-gatherer bands. In these small-scale societies, potential subordinates find ways to form robust alliances and punish would-be dominators, enforcing a form of (limited) egalitarianism.[48] Depending on the severity of the threat they pose, individuals who seek to gain excessive power might be punished mildly, through ridicule, or harshly, through non-cooperation or expulsion. In some cases, they might be punished by execution.[49] Weapons contribute to the success of anti-alpha coalitions: once the use of weapons became widespread in our ancestors, body strength became less important, since even the strongest individual could be easily overpowered by a small, armed coalition of weaker group members.[50]

Although rank-and-file coalitions are occasionally observed in some non-human primates, they are rare, fragile, and short-lived in those species.[51] Boehm suggests that, in Late Pleistocene humans anti-alpha quasi-egalitarian coalitions became common, partly through the cultural transmission of anti-alpha norms.[52] He argues that the transgenerational stability of these coalitions produced genetic selection effects.[53] Coalitionary behaviors like those described by Boehm can generate selection pressures against certain forms of aggression. According to Richard Wrangham, the execution of violent would-be alphas had a significant impact on our genetic evolution.[54] By eliminating certain genes from the human gene pool, the executions led to important changes in human bodies and brains, as well as to forms of docility that are nowadays statistically typical in our species.[55]

Sarah Blaffer Hrdy argues that women's individual and collective behavior—motivated primarily by the desire for resources and freedom—had a significant impact on the genetic evolution of human cooperative structures. Partly as a result of female strategies, our Paleolithic ancestors experienced selection for cooperative childcare. Most human children today quickly develop sophisticated mindreading skills. This is partly because the children of our ancestors had to attract the attention (and influence the behavior) not just of their mothers but also of their *allomothers* and, more generally, *alloparents*. Hrdy posits that women's spread-the-childcare-burden strategies produced changes in gene frequencies that are reflected in phenotypic traits now common in our species.[56]

Chris Knight suggests that, in ancestral hunter-gatherer bands, coalitions of women were able to control access to sexual pleasure and reproductive opportunities. Women did this through sex strikes (and related tactics), which enabled them to induce cooperation from most males. Knight maintains that certain kinds of informational exchanges, crucial for complex culture, only became possible when these female political coalitions succeeded in imposing peace within human groups.[57] Consider Hobbes's idea that stable and efficient forms of social production can occur only when there is some kind of sovereign power that imposes peaceful stability. Knight argues that coalitions of women (the "associated producers" of sexual pleasure) were able to impose on human groups the stability that permitted access to symbolic culture and all the goods that flow from it. It was, says Knight, the original "human revolution": the one that distanced us from the other apes.[58] This form of female power could impact not just social norms and expectations but genetic fitness as well. The frequency of genes contributing to specific types of violent uncooperative behavior decreased.[59]

All these narratives face problems and objections.[60] But, again, we can focus on a general issue rather than on controversial details. What is important in this context is this idea, which is supported by ample evidence: human praxis can change human bodies, minds, and societies in many ways; one of these ways is the production of selection pressures that affect human gene frequencies. Human praxis, including political praxis, can alter what Marx calls "the ensemble of social relations." Significant changes in social relations can lead to a multitude of other transformations; in some cases, they can lead to changes in the human gene pool.

*

Human nature is not limited to statistically typical traits; nor is it limited to traits unaffected by human culture and praxis. Human nature encompasses all our important phenotypic and genetic traits and differences, including those traits and differences that are partly shaped (developmentally or evolutionarily) by human social doings and cultural dynamics.[61] Is this way of thinking about human nature too permissive?[62] It is only as permissive as the criteria we choose to identify those "corporeal and mental endowments" that are important (or fundamental) in the context of scientific theorizing about humans or in the context of conversations and decisions about human futures.[63] Besides important "biological" traits and differences, should we make room for other things too within our concept of human nature? The answer to this question depends on how exactly we want to "rationally regulate" the interactions between ideas about what we fundamentally are and our conversations and decisions about human futures.[64] Even if we decide to give a negative answer and restrict our focus of attention, some skeptics might argue that the proposed approach deviates too much from standard ways of thinking about human nature and that this deviation implicitly amounts to an eliminativist stance. To these skeptics, a response can be offered in the spirit of Marx's non-eliminativist claims: a critique of common ways of thinking about human nature can help us dissolve some misguided and pernicious disputes, but this critique should not necessarily lead us to abandon the language of human nature, which remains a valuable resource.

It is true that debates about what we fundamentally are do not need to be articulated in the language of human nature; *the human condition* and other expressions can be used. However, we should keep in mind that the language of human nature has a long history of being used to express views about some aspects of what we fundamentally are. Furthermore, our cumulatively evolving understanding of nature makes the language of human nature well-suited for scientifically informed discussions about what we fundamentally are. Discussions about what we fundamentally are will not go away, and the language of human nature can helpfully connect these discussions (or at least some of them) to some parts of the sciences of nature.

Our Common Humanity

Central to Darwin's thinking about human variation was the debate about human "races" between "monogenists" (or "unitarists") and "polygenists" (or "pluralists"). Monogenists claimed that human "races" were all part of a single species with a single origin; polygenists claimed that human "races" were separate species with separate origins. The single-species thesis was favored by anti-slavery abolitionists, while the many-species thesis was favored by slavery supporters and seen as a possible justification for slavery. Darwin grew up in a fervently abolitionist family and became a fervent abolitionist himself.[65]

In *The Descent of Man and Selection in Relation to Sex*, one of the arguments that Darwin puts forward in support of the single-species thesis is that the differences between human racial groups grade into each other without gaps, just like many of the differences he had observed in other species, barnacles included:

> Every naturalist who has had the misfortune to undertake the description of a group of highly varying organisms, has encountered cases (I speak after experience) precisely like that of man; and if of a cautious disposition, he will end by uniting all the forms which graduate into each other as a single species.[66]

Darwin proposes to use sexual selection to explain the "external differences between the races"—traits such as skin color and odor, hair color and texture, the shape of the lips, ears, skull, hips, and so forth. These "external differences" cannot be due to natural selection because, he argues, they do not in general appear to be adaptations of different human groups to local conditions.[67] However, the "external differences" can be easily explained once it is acknowledged that different human societies hold different standards of physical beauty, and that these standards play a role in the choice of sexual partners. If those considered more physically attractive are more reproductively successful, and if what is physically attractive in one population is different from what is attractive in another population, there can be evolutionary divergence. For instance, if darker skin is perceived as beautiful in one group, it will become more common in that group; if in another group it is perceived as unappealing, it will become less common. Provided there are hereditary mechanisms that make preferences of this sort sufficiently stable, two populations can evolve in different directions: darker skin in one, lighter skin in the other.[68]

Darwin is aware that aesthetic standards can result in evolutionary divergence thanks to his study of animal breeding, and pigeon fancying in particular. By ensuring that only pigeons with certain observable features are allowed to reproduce, breeders can artificially select for desired traits. Breeders with different standards or goals can bring about evolutionary divergence in pigeon traits through artificial selection. Human sexual selection operates as an "unconscious" form of artificial selection.[69]

Darwin suggests that there are no objective (nonrelative) standards for ranking human "races" according to their beauty. Beauty is in the eye of the beholder. But Darwin is not willing to say the same about population differences in "mental endowments." The differences in "intellectual and moral or social faculties" are not to be treated like the differences in "external characters."[70] He presents various hypotheses about the evolution by natural selection of the "noble qualities," including "sympathy which feels for the most debased," "benevolence which extends not only to other men but to the humblest living creature," and the "god-like intellect which has penetrated into the movements and constitution of the solar system."[71] These "noble qualities" are generally found in their highest form only in "civilised races," and their evolution is due to natural rather than sexual selection.

About the Indigenous peoples of Tierra del Fuego, whom he met during his journey on the *HMS Beagle*, Darwin shockingly writes:

> The astonishment which I felt on first seeing a party of Fuegians on a wild and broken shore will never be forgotten by me, for the reflection at once rushed into my mind—such were our ancestors. These men were absolutely naked and bedaubed with paint, their long hair was tangled, their mouths frothed with excitement, and their expression was wild, startled, and distrustful. They possessed hardly any arts, and like wild animals lived on what they could catch; they had no government, and were merciless to every one not of their own small tribe. He who has seen a savage in his native land will not feel much shame, if forced to acknowledge that the blood of some more humble creature flows in his veins. For my own part I would as soon be descended from that heroic little monkey, who braved his dreaded enemy in order to save the life of his keeper; or from that old baboon, who, descending from the mountains, carried away in triumph his young comrade from a crowd of astonished dogs—as from a savage who delights to torture his enemies, offers up bloody sacrifices, practises infanticide without remorse, treats his wives like slaves, knows no decency, and is haunted by the grossest superstitions.[72]

The Fuegians, according to Darwin, appear aesthetically unpleasant to "civilised" people, something that can be explained by appeal to disagreements in aesthetic standards and the operation of sexual selection. However, the intellectual, moral, and political "inferiority" of the Fuegians cannot, in his view, be explained in the same way, and it is not merely a matter of taste. It is what Darwin perceives as the Fuegians's moral depravity that bothers him the most. He even suggests that the Fuegians are further removed from what is morally required (rather than from a biologically defined ideal type) than are some nonhuman individuals.

Darwin also criticizes the Fuegians for being too politically egalitarian.[73] The Fuegians are full members of the human species, but morally and politically they are not how humans ought to be. There are passages where Darwin refers to the Fuegians to emphasize the similarities in mental faculties across human populations. The passages where he focuses on what he perceives as the inferiority of the Fuegians are about them in their home environment. In contrast, when Darwin speaks of the similarities between the Fuegians and "civilised races," he mentions those Fuegians who were captured, brought to England, and later returned to Tierra del Fuego:

> The Fuegians rank amongst the lowest barbarians; but I was continually struck with surprise how closely the three natives on board HMS Beagle, who had lived some years in England and could talk a little English, resembled us in disposition and in most of our mental faculties.[74]

The way the Fuegians were represented in the *Beagle* narratives can be seen in Figure 2.

*

Darwin discusses how civilization and the level of intelligence that accompanies it enable "sympathy" to be "extended" to all humans, irrespective of "race," and even to non-human ("lower") creatures.[75] Even though this extension is possible, he says, racial genocide is probably inevitable:

> At some future period, not very distant as measured by centuries, the civilised races of man will almost certainly exterminate and replace throughout the world the savage races.[76]

Figure 2 *Frontispiece of FitzRoy 1839. For details about the Indigenous populations of Tierra del Fuego, and the history of encounters between these populations and European explorers and settlers (as well as the negative impact that these encounters had on the Indigenous), see the work of Anne Chapman (2010), which tries to "situate the [Fuegian populations] in universal history as relevant actors in these last four centuries" (p. 5). About this frontispiece, Chapman writes: "This man looks like Jemmy Button in 1834, when FitzRoy [the Beagle's Captain] and Darwin returned to say goodbye to him" (p. 234). Jemmy Button was, in fact, Orundellico, one of the hostages who were taken to England and then back to Tierra del Fuego. Darwin was surprised to see "Jemmy" revert to his "savage" modes of life upon his return (Darwin 1845, pp. 228–9). Image courtesy of Houghton Library, *75–836, seq. 688.*

Humans have acquired the "noble qualities" that are absent or rare in the lower animals through conflicts and competitions at the group level.[77] These conflicts and competitions are also responsible, according to Darwin, for what he sees as the success of "civilised races" over the "inferior" ones.

It is useful to also read those infamous passages in *Descent* where Darwin discusses the intellectual and moral differences not between "civilised races" and "savages," but rather within "civilised countries." These are the sections where he writes about the "the weak members of civilised societies," "the very poor and reckless, who are often degraded by vice," "the reckless, degraded, and often vicious members of society," and "the reckless, the vicious and otherwise inferior members of society." These individuals, says Darwin, "tend to increase at a quicker rate than the provident and generally virtuous members."[78]

In these passages, Darwin is responding to claims made by Francis Galton, his younger half-cousin. Galton had argued for the need to facilitate the reproduction of the better members of society and curb the "multiplication" of the less useful members of society. After Darwin's death, Galton went on to coin the term "eugenics," which he defined as "the improvement of inborn qualities, or stock."[79] Galtonian views ended up shaping many eugenic policies around the world in the first part of the twentieth century. In *Descent*, written before eugenic ideas became popular, Darwin maintains that, even without the intervention of social engineers, there are barriers that slow "the multiplication of the reckless and improvident":

> Malefactors are executed, or imprisoned for long periods, so that they cannot freely transmit their bad qualities. Melancholic and insane persons are confined, or commit suicide. Violent and quarrelsome men often come to a bloody end. […] Profligate women bear few children, and profligate men rarely marry; both suffer from disease.[80]

Darwin argues that these reproductive "checks" might not be enough, and that when the checks fail "the nation will retrograde, as has occurred too often in the history of the world." According to the English naturalist:

> We must remember that progress is no invariable rule [...] Development of all kinds depends on many concurrent favourable circumstances.[81]

Evolution by natural selection does not inevitably lead to intellectually and morally valuable things. Identifying the conditions that can bring about intellectual and moral improvement is a challenging task. Darwin cautions against policies aimed at punishing the "helpless." Such policies are likely to be counterproductive, negatively impacting some of our morally superior tendencies. Making it harder for the "weak" to survive and reproduce is not a coherent way to promote progress:

> The aid which we feel impelled to give to the helpless is mainly an incidental result of the instinct of sympathy [...]. Nor could we check our sympathy, if so urged by hard reason, without deterioration in the noblest part of our nature. [...] If we were intentionally to neglect the weak and helpless, it could only be for a contingent benefit, with a certain and great present evil. Hence we must bear without complaining the undoubtedly bad effects of the weak surviving and propagating their kind.[82]

*

Even though he disliked his cousin's interventionist zeal, Darwin's morals and politics were undoubtedly shaped by the racist and classist attitudes that were common among the nineteenth-century British elites. While his biases differ in some respects from those of Galton, they are nonetheless evident.[83] Scientific theorizing is never pure, and Darwin's work was no exception. Nevertheless, we can endorse a Darwinian tree-of-life-and-ubiquitous-variation framework without accepting Darwin's moral and political views. In our own impure ways, we can pull apart different aspects of his conception of the world and walk away with those that we find most useful.

It is also important to stress that various scientific hypotheses put forward by Darwin have turned out to be wrong. According to current accounts, for example, differences in skin color evolved in response to selection pressures for photoprotection and for the enabling of vitamin D synthesis, not as a result of sexual selection (although sexual selection theory has proven useful in other contexts).[84] As for the notion of "race," the available evidence from molecular studies and other sources indicates that humans cannot be divided into genetically defined clusters that align with "race" categories. In an important sense, races do not exist.[85] Diversity in skin color and (culturally constructed) racialized identities should be seen as part of our current human nature, whereas races with inherited genetic foundations, arguably, should not.

*

A view according to which important dimensions of genetic and phenotypic variation are part of what we fundamentally are can, in principle, be embraced by individuals with radically different evaluative standards and political projects. For instance, it can be embraced by someone who argues that the conditions currently labeled as "disabilities" are a source of social wealth and value; it can also be embraced by someone who argues that these very same conditions are a source of social disvalue, a burden to be removed. The view can be embraced by Marx-inspired egalitarians, but also by Nietzsche-inspired inegalitarians. In principle, these egalitarians and inegalitarians could agree on what important traits and differences are found in humans, and they might even be willing to rely on identical descriptions of such traits and differences. The egalitarians could assert that these differences should be celebrated but that the social and economic inequalities associated with them should be leveled. The inegalitarians could instead assert that the differences should be used to organize society hierarchically: a small group of exceptional individuals should be at the top, in charge of creating great new values, and a large group of inferior individuals should be at the bottom, with the sole function of supporting—and serving as tools of—those at the top. The egalitarians could claim that we should embrace modes of life in which "the free development of each is the condition for the free development of all"; the inegalitarians could claim that exceptional individuals should have "the monopoly of development," in the sense that the "free development" of exceptional individuals should have priority over everyone else's development.[86]

As soon as differences become salient, ranking and counter-ranking become tempting. This often leads to differences being depicted in evaluatively loaded terms. Nonetheless, we can find ways to make our conversations on human futures more transparent, even though not necessarily less ideological.

*

Many nowadays place the idea of moral equality at the center of their moral and political vision. The assumption that moral equality can be grounded in a species-invariant phenotypic essence should be abandoned: such an essence does not exist. Various religious traditions suggest that humans are different in all sorts of ways but equal *before God*. But how can one justify in non-religious terms a belief in human moral equality, given our biocultural diversity?[87]

Darwin thought that a bio-genealogically defined common humanity could be used in support of—or at least as a motivation for—the abolition of slavery. However, a bio-genealogically defined common humanity is compatible with the view that some humans are morally superior and some morally inferior. Humans are all "netted together," but so are all living beings.[88] Darwin writes that "humanity to the lower animals" can, in general, only be found in the noblest humans and is rare among the "savages." His hatred of slavery was rooted in his aversion to cruelty to animals, rather than in a belief in human moral equality. According to Darwin, humans are morally worthy to different degrees, and some non-human individuals—such as the "heroic little monkey" who saves his keeper and the "old baboon" who saves his friend—are morally worthier than some human individuals. After Darwin's death, one of his sons recalled that the "two subjects which moved my father perhaps more deeply than any others were cruelty to animals and slavery—his detestation of both was intense, and his indignation was overwhelming in case of any levity or want of feeling on these matters."[89]

Darwin cannot give us the political and moral tools we need. But a Darwinian framework for thinking about human variation might lead us to the view that the focus should be not on moral equality per se, understood in standard static ways, but rather on an idea or ideal of a common humanity that goes beyond bio-genealogical ancestor-sharing. Instead of seeking common humanity in the nonexistent "Man in general," we might see it as something to be constructed—as something that, among other things, requires human praxis.[90] There are different ways of elaborating this suggestion. One Marx-inspired way consists in claiming that bringing about our common humanity coincides with the movement toward human modes of life with specific characteristics: we need to piece together human differences so that, increasingly, the free development of each can contribute to the free development of all. A Marx-inspired perspective allows one to see that the construction of a common humanity involves the creation of new technologies, new institutions, new conceptions of the world, new ways of regulating our "social metabolism" and our "interchange with nature," as well as new "struggles" among antagonistic social groups.[91] In any case, what is important here is that this idea/ideal of a common humanity does not require abandoning the language of human nature. It does not require denying the important ways in which biology and other natural sciences can help us think about ourselves collectively, as members of a diverse and mutable animal species, living alongside other species on a very peculiar planet.[92]

Conclusions

In *The German Ideology*, Marx and Engels refer to our human "modes of life" and say that these comprise our "modes of production," which are the ways in which humans "daily re-create their own life" and "propagate" their kind. Marx and Engels argue that every human mode of life is "conditioned" by the human "corporeal organisation," which they also call "physical constitution." This "corporeal organisation" affects the way we produce human goods and therefore also our "relation with the rest of nature." Moreover, they argue, human modes of life are affected by the "natural conditions in which humans find themselves, geological, oro-hydrographical, climatic, and so on."[1]

In his formulation of the philosophy of praxis, Gramsci does not properly come to terms with the ways in which human bodies and the rest of nature condition our modes of life. The philosophy of praxis must acknowledge the transformative impact of human doings and thinkings, but it must also pay close attention to the human corporeal organization and to all the extracorporeal contexts in which our doings and thinkings occur.

Gramsci points out that the philosophy of praxis is a philosophy "not of the 'pure act' but rather of the 'impure'—that is, the real—act, in the secular sense of the word."[2] But how impure is this act? He writes:

> Is the "human"—as a concept and as a unitary fact—a starting point or a point of arrival? Or, rather, isn't the attempt to posit the "human" as a starting point a "theological" and "metaphysical" residue? [...] The unity of humankind is not given by the "biological" nature of man. In history, the human differences that matter are not reducible to biology. [...] Furthermore, "biological unity" has never counted for much in history. [...] Nor [can] the "faculty of reason" or the "mind" [...] be regarded as a unitary fact. [...] That "human nature" is the "ensemble of social relations" is the most satisfying answer, because it includes the idea of becoming—man becomes, he changes continuously with the changing of social relations—and because it negates "man in general." Indeed, social relations are expressed by diverse groups of men that presuppose one another, and their unity is dialectical, not formal. [...] One could also say that the nature of man is "history" (and, in this sense, since history = spirit, that the nature of man is the spirit), if history is taken to mean, precisely, "becoming" in a "concordia discors" that does not have unity for its point of departure but contains in itself the reasons for a possible unity. Therefore, "human nature" cannot be found in any particular human being but in the entire history of the human species (and the use of the word "species," with its naturalistic timbre, is itself significant).[3]

Here, Gramsci is presenting his own version of the Marxian rejection of the myth of the "man in general" and of the idea that our common humanity is something to be constructed, a point of arrival and not of departure. He suggests that biological and psychological similarities and differences do not count for much, even if it is the case that we use biological terms to speak about humans. Gramsci identifies human nature with human history, which he understands in terms of human praxis, but without any proper reference to how such praxis is conditioned by the "corporeal organisation" and the "natural conditions" ("geological, oro-hydrographical, climatic, and so on"). He invokes the sixth of Marx's *Theses on Feuerbach*, according to which "the essence of man [...] is the ensemble of the social relations."[4] What the sixth thesis actually means—and whether it can be reconciled with what *The German Ideology* says about the corporeal organization and the natural conditions—is a complex issue that cannot be addressed here. Regardless, the way Gramsci uses the sixth thesis within his own reflection, as Timpanaro points out, concedes too much to anti-materialist views.[5]

Gramsci claims that, among the relations that fundamentally constitute us, there are our relations with nature and not just our relations with other humans. However, he says, our relations with nature (and thereby also with our own natural bodies) are always already mediated by our relations with other humans; moreover, while some of our relations with nature might be non-voluntary, they are always already affected by our being conscious of them and by our activities.[6] This approach makes room for nature only as an object of our actions and thoughts.[7] Timpanaro writes:

> Man is not, according to the definition that Gramsci prefers and takes as basic, *only* an ensemble of social relations. Man is also animality, biologicality. Obviously, the social relations are not mere *additions* to our animality: they have reacted onto it, they have partly modified and reshaped it; *in this sense*, the social relations have overcome such animality. But if by "overcome" one means negated and reduced to mere prehistorical antecedent (and this is what Gramsci meant, despite some oscillations, which he himself minimized), too many fundamental aspects of the human condition are arbitrarily set aside.[8]

Gramsci's reading of Marx's third thesis on Feuerbach also deserves to be mentioned. Marx asserts that there is a "coincidence of the changing of circumstances and of human activity or self-change."

He claims that this coincidence "can be conceived and rationally understood only as revolutionary praxis." The German phrase Marx uses is "*revolutionäre Praxis.*" The theses were first published in a version edited by Engels, which was the version Gramsci had access to; in Engels's rendition, Marx's phrase is substituted with "*umwälzende Praxis*" (praxis that overturns, overturning praxis). Gramsci translates Engels's words into Italian as "*il rovesciamento della praxis*" (the overturning of praxis). In this way, Gramsci directs the reader's attention to the ways in which praxis can be overturned and can overturn itself and, at least to some extent, away from the ways in which praxis can overturn the rest of reality in general.[9]

*

Labriola's distinction between "living in nature" and "living in society" is undoubtedly simplistic. Ordinary intuitions about which aspects of reality are likely to resist our transformative efforts are unreliable. There are aspects of reality that precede and preexist human praxis and that, until now, have not been affected by it. There are also aspects of reality that have been modified by human praxis but remain beyond human control. Only some small fragments of our niche construction are the desired and intended results of our individual or collective plans. This is something that Engels emphasizes:

> Let us not [...] flatter ourselves overmuch on account of our human victories over nature. For each such victory nature takes its revenge on us. Each victory, it is true, in the first place brings about the results we expected, but in the second and third places it has quite different, unforeseen effects which only too often cancel the first. [...] Thus at every step we are reminded that we by no means rule over nature like a conqueror over a foreign people, like someone standing outside nature—but that we, with flesh, blood and brain, belong to nature, and exist in its midst, and that all our mastery

> of it consists in the fact that we have the advantage over all other creatures of being able to learn its laws and apply them correctly.[10]

Timpanaro points out that Engels saw clearly the need to fuse a socioeconomic historico-materialist perspective with the natural sciences:

> Even more than by Marx [...] the need for the construction of a materialism which was not purely socio-economic but also 'natural' was felt by Engels, and this was a great merit of his. The impulse to deepen their materialism in this way came not only from the general philosophical and scientific climate of the second half of the nineteenth century, but more specifically from the radical change which Darwinism introduced in the natural sciences, by its definitive demonstration [...] of the historicity of nature. The task was now no longer to counterpose the historicity of human society to the ahistoricity of nature, but to establish both the linkage and the distinction between the two historicities.[11]

Timpanaro insightfully argues that Engels's materialism is in some respects nondialectical, as it properly acknowledges the occurrence of "unmitigated losses [*perdite secche*]" in our interactions with our own bodies and with our biotic and abiotic surroundings.[12] Some of the ways in which both the human and the non-human parts of nature frustrate our desires and hopes will not be dialectically overcome.[13] Even if we became capable of unleashing our productive potentials by reorganizing our societies along communist lines, our triumph would not be complete. As Timpanaro puts it, nature would "continue to be a cause of unhappiness even in communist society."[14] Only a perspective that properly integrates the findings of the natural sciences within our worldview, and that provides good tools for studying the interactions between human praxis and its corporeal and extracorporeal settings, can help us identify, make sense, and come to terms with these "unmitigated losses."

The relevant integrations should avoid any *scientistic* fanfare.[15] Misleading simplifications are a constant danger in scientific discourses that take humans as their object of study, and biological and evolutionary approaches have often produced and promoted such simplifications. Scientific research on humans is never disinterested, partly because of its impact on human praxis. Gramsci rejects any "superficial infatuation with science," and rightly so. He is aware that this "infatuation" hinders various forms of liberatory praxis and that the "superstitious faith" in science leads to political "impotence."[16] But Gramsci wants his philosophy of liberatory praxis—and the account of what we fundamentally are that comes with it—to be self-sufficient, and this assertion of self-sufficiency takes him away from the kinds of integrations that an Engelsian standpoint recommends.[17]

In the days before he was arrested by Mussolini's fascist police, Gramsci was working on an essay about "the Southern question."[18] In this unfinished essay, he discusses the way various Italian intellectuals, both right-wing and left-wing, had used "scientific" ideas as a tool for governing, oppressing, and exploiting the masses, and for discouraging any alliance between the workers of the Italian North and the peasants of the Italian South:

> It is well known what kind of ideology has been disseminated in myriad ways among the masses in the North, by propagandists of the bourgeoisie: the South is the ball and chain which prevents the social development of Italy from progressing more rapidly; the Southerners are biologically inferior beings, semi-barbarians or total barbarians, by natural destiny; if the South is backward, the fault does not lie with the capitalist system or with any other historical cause, but with Nature, which has made the Southerners

> lazy, incapable, criminal and barbaric—only tempering this harsh fate with the purely individual explosion of a few great geniuses, like isolated palm trees in an arid and barren desert. The Socialist party was to a great extent the vehicle for this bourgeois ideology within the Northern proletariat. [...] Once again, "science" was used to crush the wretched and exploited; but this time it was dressed in socialist colours, and claimed to be the science of the proletariat.[19]

In his prison notebooks, Gramsci deplores the "widespread opinion" according to which "if the South made no progress [...], this meant that the causes of the poverty were not external but internal; moreover, given the deep-seated belief in the great natural wealth of the land, there remained but one explanation: the organic incapacity of the people, their barbarity, their biological inferiority."[20]

Born and raised in Sardinia, one of the poorest regions of the Italian South, Gramsci suffered physically and mentally as a result of economic deprivation. He witnessed directly how scientific and pseudo-scientific discourses about human differences—concerning the ability of populations to govern themselves rationally—could be manufactured and manipulated to serve the interests of ruthless elites.[21] He even accused the Italian government and capitalists of exploiting Sardinia more than they exploited the Italian colonies in Africa.[22] Timpanaro's suggestion that Gramsci's "attenuation of materialism" was due to "cultural contingencies of the milieu in which he lived" mistakenly downplays the philosophical significance of some of these "contingencies." It is through a complex mix of personal (even corporeal) and theoretical reasons that the Sardinian communist philosopher was able to grasp the importance of combating the notion of barbarian populations, irrational by nature and in need of external governance. It would be simplistic to claim that Gramsci's "attenuation of materialism" was nothing but an overreaction to materialistic approaches deployed to justify and reinforce those inequalities that he hated and wanted to destroy. And yet, it seems that the focus on the role of natural science in relation to certain forms of oppression created hole (a sort of blind spot) in Gramsci's view.[23]

The fact that we (most of us) have ideas about human nature, which affect the way we think, act, and live, is important. Having ideas about human nature (with certain kinds of causal powers) is part of human nature (in its current form). A Gramscian framework can help us understand the "ideological" role played by such ideas, which are components of what Gramsci refers to as "conceptions of the world."[24] Those "infatuated" with science often fail to grasp this ideological role, which is frequently exploited by those aiming to infatuate their audience. Nonetheless, anti-science ways of intervening in conversations and decisions about human futures—and therefore anti-materialistic attempts to overturn praxis—are ultimately bound to fail.

*

In *The Eighteenth Brumaire*, Marx writes:

> Men make their own history, but they do not make it just as they please; they do not make it under circumstances chosen by themselves, but under circumstances directly encountered, given and transmitted from the past.[25]

As the rest of the passage indicates, the "circumstances" Marx is referring to are specific politico-cultural models and events.[26] A fully Engelsian Marx, eager to develop his socioeconomic materialism within a broader corporeal, ecological, and cosmic materialism, could have used these words in a more general sense. Each generation of humans makes history under circumstances inherited from the past. Among such circumstances, there are some that have been "conditioned"—that have been niche-constructed—by the actions and thoughts of previous generations, and some that have not. This applies to our biotic and abiotic surroundings, but it also applies to our "corporeal and mental endowments" and to the patterns of variation in relation to such "endowments." These "endowments" and patterns of variation are "given and transmitted from the past." They are often unwanted and in need of "overturning."

Debates about human nature have often been framed as debates between what we might call the *limitationists* and the *potentialists*. By pointing to alleged "zones of improbable or forbidden entry," the limitationists claim that human nature frustrates and renders ineffective attempts at radical change.[27] In contrast, the potentialists declare that human nature contains many as yet unexpressed potentialities, whose manifestation (or actualization) we can bring about through social praxis.[28] At an abstract level, the disagreement between these two factions does not make much sense, since it is obvious that human "endowments," with their variants and distributions, contextually contribute to determining what is currently within our reach, and what is not. The disagreement starts making sense only when specific goals are considered. Once we have provisionally identified a desirable goal, we can begin reflecting on whether the current ("given") circumstances—those under which we make our history—are conducive to achieving this goal. If the circumstances make the goal difficult to attain, we can try to establish whether and in what ways we can change these circumstances, what might be the costs of making these changes, whether there are ways to bypass the "given" circumstances, and so on. Such reflections can lead us to reshape—and in some cases "overturn"—our praxis and goals.

Some politically motivated skeptics are worried by the way the language of human nature can be used to discourage liberatory and revolutionary praxis. They fear that accepting this language means letting the limitationists win. This fear, as suggested by Marx's strategy, can be kept at bay by embracing and promoting better ways of thinking about the circumstances under which we make our own history.

Some human "endowments" are phylogenetically and historically old, while others are recent; but this does not tell us how difficult it is to alter them. Sex differences at the genital level are evolutionarily old, but current techno-scientific advancements offer new transformative tools in this area; alongside these tools come new opportunities and risks that arise as individuals, public institutions, and private companies gain access to the relevant technologies.[29] In contrast, the psychocultural differences that are causally intertwined with global inequalities in the distribution of both economic and noneconomic goods could, for all we know, prove more challenging to modify than one might have anticipated—or hoped for. These are just examples and what we think about them could swiftly change as our understanding of the relevant details evolves. More important than any specific case is the general framework we decide to adopt. The way we think about our "endowments" is a structural element of this framework. We should not assume that intervening directly at a molecular level is more difficult than intervening at a cultural level, nor should we assume that the opposite is true. We should acknowledge that our intuitions about what traits and differences are easy or difficult to change are often mistaken.

We need to avoid simplistic ways of conceiving of the interactions among genetic structures, phenotypic traits, and human praxis. What we are learning about niche-construction dynamics can help us to better grasp the "linkage and the distinction" between human praxis and its material context—corporeal and extracorporeal, economic and ecologic, planetary and cosmic.

*

In a work titled *Zoonomia*, Charles Darwin's grandfather, Erasmus, draws attention to the similarities between humans and worms:

Go, proud reasoner, and call the worm thy sister![30]

Much like humans, earthworms make history under circumstances not of their choosing, "given and transmitted from the past." The niche-constructing activities of earthworms interact with those of many other species, much as ours do. We, however, cumulatively construct collective ways of thinking about ourselves and the world; earthworms do not do this. Earthworms "overturn" the soil; we collectively "overturn" many aspects of reality, including our social relations, our conceptions of the world, and our ideas about our own nature. Fully grasping the similarities and differences between us and the earthworms (and the barnacles, the bees, the ants, the cranes, and so on) can be a source of tools for "overturning" human praxis.

*

> Only people immersed in the day-to-day minutiae of politics could fail to notice that the immense transformations going on in the world today, for good or ill, were all born in the laboratory. New forms of farming, new weapons, new illnesses and new cures, new sources of energy and new contaminations.[31]

This is from an interview to Primo Levi. In some important ways, what Levi is arguing here is wrong. Many of the transformations of nature (human and non-human) that are going on today, or that will occur in the near future, have deep roots in our biocultural history. These roots include phenotypic traits that our ancestors acquired a long time ago, such as smaller teeth, reduced levels aggression, and mindreading skills. Moreover, many of these transformations are shaped by fragments of human social praxis currently happening not in science labs but rather in workplaces, financial markets, government palaces, art galleries, street protests, social media platforms, and various other contexts. Nevertheless, Levi is correct in noting that many of these significant transformations are made possible, triggered, or shaped by the findings (and more generally the research activities of individuals, groups, and institutions) in the natural sciences.

*

Human nature matters because it is part of the *circumstances under which we make our own history*. Human nature is not *fixed and immutable*. Human praxis can transform human nature, and often does. As human praxis changes, the ways human nature is transformed change too. Human history is, among other things, *a continuous transformation of human nature*. By *acting on the world*, we *at the same time change our nature*. Steering the transformations of human nature in specific directions is difficult as well as risky. Our culturally driven niche-constructing activities generate *unforeseen effects*, and there are *uncontrolled forces* that affect our modes of life. Human *free development* requires *favorable circumstances*, and progress is *no invariable rule*. But the transformative processes cannot be stopped, and we need to decide how to deal with them, or at least what attitudes to have toward them.

Notes

Introduction

1 Labriola 1903, pp. 220–1, translation modified; Labriola 1965, pp. 135–6 [*Del materialismo storico: dilucidazione preliminare*]; "artificial terrain" translates "*terreno artificiale.*" See also Labriola 1903, p. 180; 1965, p. 112.

2 "The philosophy of praxis [...] is the pith [*midollo*, marrow] of historical materialism" (Labriola 1907, p. 60, translation modified; 1965, p. 216 [*Discorrendo di socialismo e di filosofia*]).

3 See Gramsci 1975a, Q4§37; Q5§127; Q7§18; Q8§22; Q8§235; Q10II§6; Q11§17; Q11§22; Q11§27; Q11§30; Q11§59; Q11§62; Q15§61; Q17§12; Q17§18. See what Gramsci says about Labriola's reformulation of historical materialism in Q4§3; Q16§9. For a discussion of the Italian debates on the philosophy of praxis from Labriola to Gramsci, see Mustè 2021; Frosini 2004; on "praxis" in Marx and the Marxist tradition, see Candioti 2022. Gramsci considers the interaction between dominant and subaltern groups as crucial for understanding historical processes; his philosophy of praxis should be understood in the light of this.

4 Timpanaro 1975, p. 56; "*attenuazione del materialismo*," Timpanaro 1970, p. 37; cf. Morera 2014.

5 According to Timpanaro, Labriola himself was "in certain respects a too impatient adversary of 'vulgar materialism'" (Timpanaro 1975, p. 49). Labriola argues that the term "scientific" is often "miserably abused" and that "scientific communism" should instead be called "critical communism" (Labriola 1903, pp. 12–13, translation modified; Labriola 1965, p. 7 [*In memoria del Manifesto dei Comunisti*]). Labriola rejects "political and social Darwinism" and criticizes those who fatalistically misconstrue the ways in which historical materialism "*naturalizes*" history (Labriola 1903, p. 113; see also p. 43; Labriola 1965, p. 72 [*Del materialismo storico*]). On the interaction between Darwinism and Marxism at the end of the nineteenth century and the beginning of the twentieth, see Stack 2003; for Marx and Engels's comments on the theory of natural selection, see Marx and Engels 1975–2004 (*Collected Works*, MECW), vol. 25, pp. 63–5, p. 331, pp. 582–5; vol. 31, p. 351; vol. 40, p. 551; vol. 41, p. 380; vol. 43, p. 529; vol. 45, pp. 106–9; and the exchange between Marx and Engels on Pierre Trémaux's evolutionary views, in vol. 42.

6 Timpanaro 1975, p. 238, p. 242, p. 56. Gramsci's motivation for many of the views contained in his prison notebooks can be better understood by considering his personal circumstances as well as his interactions with the Italian Communist Party and events in the Soviet Union; cf. Rossi 2014; Ghetti 2014.

7 Timpanaro 1982, pp. 301–2 (cf. p. 244, and p. 289). My translation; the term "coarseness" translates "*rozzezza*," a term that Gramsci uses in the notebooks to refer to lack of cultural sophistication and intellectual depth; on "good sense" (and "common sense") in Gramsci, see Liguori 2009. See also Timpanaro 2001, ch. 11. On determinism and history, see the final essay in Timpanaro 1982.

8 See for example Q4§40; Q4§32; Q9§131; Q8§205; Q11§14, Q11§20; Q11§22; see also "vulgar evolutionism" in Q11§9, Q11§26.

9 See for example Q11§12.

10 Gramsci 1992–2007, vol. 3, p. 195, Q7§47. In Q4§3 (Q16§9), Gramsci writes that "popular religion is crassly materialistic" (Gramsci 1992–2007, vol. 2, p. 143). In one of his early works, Gramsci writes: "What can be historicized cannot be supernatural in origin, the vestige of some divine revelation. [...] Our religion becomes, once again, history. Our faith becomes, once again, man, and man's will and his capacity for action" (Gramsci 1994, p. 14; "La storia," 1916, in Gramsci 1960, p. 142).

11 Timpanaro 1975, p. 101, p. 118, p. 238. Timpanaro discusses what he sees as the "anti-materialist phobia" and "anti-biological phobia" of Western Marxism (Timpanaro 1975, pp. 22–31, p. 58, p. 214; see also his multi-floor house metaphor on pp. 44–5; for a discussion see Losurdo 2010; Gedik 2022). Timpanaro characterizes materialism in this way: "By materialism we understand above all acknowledgement of the priority of nature over 'mind', or if you like, of the physical level over the biological level, and of the biological over the socio-economic and cultural level; both in the sense of chronological priority (the very long time which supervened before life appeared on earth, and between the origin of life and the origin of man), and in the sense of the conditioning which nature *still* exercises on man and will continue to exercise at least for the foreseeable future. Cognitively, therefore, the materialist maintains that experience cannot be reduced either to production of reality by a subject (however such production is conceived) or to a reciprocal implication of subject and object. We cannot, in other words, deny or evade the element of passivity in experience: the external situation which we do not create but which imposes itself on us. Nor can we in any way reabsorb this external datum by making it a mere negative moment in the activity of the subject, or by making both the subject and the object mere moments, distinguishable only in abstraction, of a single effective reality" (Timpanaro 1975, p. 34). Much could be said on how this way of thinking about materialism relates to other perspectives on materialism. We cannot delve into this intricate set of issues here; what is crucial for our purposes can be summarized as follows: there are parts and aspects of reality that precede (or preexist) human praxis; there are parts and aspects of reality that are not in any way constituted by human praxis; there are parts and aspects of reality that (until now) have not been modified by human praxis; there are parts and aspects of reality that, despite being affected by human praxis, remain beyond human control; the natural sciences generate useful cognitive tools for grappling with all these parts and aspects of reality.

12 Different appropriations of the phrase "philosophy of praxis" are possible; cf. Finelli 1999; Thomas 2009; Feenberg 2014. The appropriation I am suggesting requires, among other things, abandoning the idea that human praxis is equivalent to the production of collective subjectivities: the latter is only one aspect among many of human praxis.

13 Odling-Smith et al. 2003, pp. 1–2; cf. Odling-Smee 1988.

14 Darwin 1881a, p. 1. See also Darwin 1838a; 1869.

15 Darwin 1881a, p. 5 and p. 313.

16 Darwin 1881a, p. 2.

17 Some influential niche-constructionist ideas can be found in Waddington 1968 and Lewontin 1983; for a discussion of Richard Lewontin's views, see Godfrey-Smith 2004. For (some of) the nineteenth-century roots of organism-environment interactionism, see Pearce 2014a; 2014b. For an expanded concept of inheritance, see the discussions in Gray 1992; 2001; and Griffiths and Gray 1994; 2001; cf. Mameli 2005.

18 Labriola 1903, p. 211, translation modified; Labriola 1965, p. 130 [*Del materialismo storico*].

19 Labriola 1903, p. 64; Labriola 1965, p. 39 [*In memoria del Manifesto dei Comunisti*]. Labriola writes that the "kernel [*nocciolo*]" of historical materialism is to be found in claims such as these: "the nature of man, his historical evolution, is in the process of *praxis*—and by saying *praxis*, under this aspect of totality, I mean the elimination of the vulgar opposition between practice and theory—for, in other words, history is the history of labor [...]; historical man is always social man, and the presumption of a presocial or supersocial man is a creature of the imagination" (Labriola 1907, p. 43, translation modified; 1965, p. 204).

20 In relation to this issue, it is important to mention Marx's notion of "species-being" (in MECW, vol. 3 [*Economic and Philosophic Manuscripts of 1844*]), although we cannot discuss the exegetical debates on that notion here.

21 Labriola 1903, p. 222, translation modified; Labriola 1965, p. 136; "ethnic character" translates "*carattere etnico.*"

22 Timpanaro 1975, pp. 49–50. On Labriola's "colonialist aberrations," see Ottaviano 1982; cf. Gramsci Q8§200 (1992–2007, vol. 3, pp. 349–50), Q11§1.

23 MECW, vol. 6, p. 192 [*Poverty of Philosophy*].

24 MECW, vol. 35, p. 187 [*Capital I*]. The (often brief and cryptic) claims on human nature offered by Marx have generated a vast debate: see, for instance, Althusser 2005; Althusser et al. 2015; Mészáros 1970; Markus 1978; McMurtry 1978; Geras 1983; Cohen and Kymlicka 1988; Lichtman 1990; Sayers 1998; Struhl 2016; Fox 2016; Fracchia 2022. I will not address the larger debate here.

25 Gramsci 1992–2007, vol. 2, p. 150, translation modified, Q4§8; Q13§20; Q6§82.

26 MECW, vol. 35, p. 187 [*Capital I*].

27 Gramsci 1992–2007, vol. 2, p. 153, Q4§11.

28 Gramsci 1971, p. 465, Q11§27. Gramsci's interpretation of Marxism is connected to his critique of positivism. A rejection of positivism is already present in his early works (cf. Losurdo 1997, ch. 2). In "Socialismo e cultura" (1916), Gramsci argues that culture is not something that "can come about through spontaneous evolution, through a series of actions and reactions which are independent of one's own will—as is the case in animal and vegetable nature, where every unit is selected and specifies its own organs unconsciously, through a fatalistic law of things. Above all, man is spirit, i.e. historical creation, not nature" (Gramsci 1977, p. 11; translation modified; Gramsci 1975b, p. 24; Gramsci 1994, p. 10). In "Il nostro Marx" (1918),

Gramsci refers to "Marxist thought, that which never dies, which is the continuation of the Italian and German idealism, and which in Marx was contaminated with positivistic and naturalistic encrustations" (Gramsci 1977, p. 34, translation modified; Gramsci 1975b, p. 150). In "Misteri della cultura e della poesia" (1918), Gramsci writes that "the fact that Marx introduced in his work some positivistic elements should not surprise and can be explained: Marx was not a professional philosopher and, occasionally, [like Homer] he nodded" (Gramsci 1975b, p. 328). In the notebooks, Gramsci changes tack and attributes the undesirable positivistic "encrustations" not to Marx himself but to "orthodox" Marxists, who have created an "inferior kind of historical materialism [*materialism storico deteriore*]," which "tends to become an ideology in the pejorative sense [*tende a diventare una ideologia nel senso deteriore*]" (Gramsci 1992–2007, vol. 3, p. 154, Q7§1; vol. 2, p. 189, Q4§40; Q11§62). These "orthodox historical materialists" have abandoned the Hegelian-Marxian insights: "Hegel [...] joined the two moments of philosophical life, materialism and spiritualism, dialectically. Hegel's successors destroyed this unity, returning to the old materialism with Feuerbach and to the spiritualism of the Hegelian right. In his youth, Marx [...] reforged the destroyed unity into a new philosophical construction [...]. Many historical materialists have done to Marx what had already been done to Hegel; in other words, they have gone from dialectical unity back to crude materialism" (Gramsci 1992–2007, vol. 2, p. 143, Q4§3; Q16§9).

29 Gramsci 1992–2007, vol. 2, p. 165, Q4§25; Q11§30.

30 Gramsci writes: "[human] history registers radical changes in social structures whereas in the case of animals one can only talk, at best, of extremely slow evolutions" (Gramsci 1992–2007, vol. 2, p. 158, Q4§15). Later in the same notebook, Gramsci adds: "it is not possible to talk about the natural history of mankind and to compare human events with natural events, other than metaphorically" (p. 189, Q4§40). In a prison letter to his eldest son, Delio, Gramsci writes: "It would seem that quantity becomes quality for man and not for other living beings" (Gramsci 1973, p. 271; letter 459 in Gramsci 1996).

Chapter 1

1 MECW, vol. 28, pp. 18 [*Economic Manuscripts of 1857–58*].

2 Smith argues that "the propensity [of the isolated individual] to truck, barter, and exchange one thing for another" is part of human nature

(Smith 1975, vol. I, ch. II, p. 25); see also Ricardo (1817). Here is what Marx writes immediately before the quoted passage: "The individual and isolated hunter and fisherman, who serves Adam Smith and Ricardo as a starting point, is one of the unimaginative fantasies of the 18th century. […] [Smith and Ricardo] saw this individual not as an historical result, but as the starting point of history; not as something evolving in the course of history, but posited by nature, because for them this individual was the natural individual, according to their idea of human nature. […] The further back we go in history, the more does the individual, and accordingly also the producing individual, appear to be dependent and belonging to a larger whole. At first, he is still in a quite natural manner part of the family, and of the family expanded into the tribe; later he is part of a community, of one of the different forms of community which arise from the conflict and the merging of tribes. It is not until the 18th century, in 'bourgeois society', that the various forms of the social nexus confront the individual as merely a means towards his private ends, as external necessity. But the epoch which produces this standpoint, that of the isolated individual, is precisely the epoch of the hitherto most highly developed social (according to this standpoint, general) relations" (MECW, vol. 28, pp. 17–18 [*Economic Manuscripts of 1857–58*]).

3 Hobbes 2012, p. 192, ch. 13.

4 Hobbes 2012, p. 192, ch. 13.

5 Hobbes 1997, p. 10 [*Preface to the Reader*] and pp. 21–6 [1.2]; Hobbes 1983, p. 90.

6 Hobbes 2012, pp. 188–90, ch. 13. See also Hobbes 1997, pp. 25–6, 1.3: "All men are equal to each other by nature." On the differences between men and women, Hobbes writes: "there is not alwayes that difference of strength, or prudence between the man and the woman as that right [of Dominion over the other] can be determined without War" (Hobbes 2012, p. 308, ch. 20); "the inequality in natural strength is too small to enable the male to acquire dominion over the female without war" (Hobbes 1997, p. 108, 9.3).

7 Hobbes 2012, p. 308, ch. 17.

8 Hobbes 2012, p. 288, ch. 19; Hobbes 1997, ch. 10.3.

9 Hobbes 2012, p. 16 [*Introduction*]. Hobbes writes that the Leviathan is an "Artificial animal," an automaton with "artificial life."

10 Hobbes 2012, p. 194, ch. 13; see also Hobbes 1997, p. 30, 1.13. On Hobbes and America, see Aravamudan 2009.

11 Hobbes 1997, p. 24, 1.2 (footnote). Hobbes continues: "Infants and the uninstructed are ignorant of their Force, and those who do not know what would be lost by the absence of Society are unaware of their usefulness. Hence the former cannot enter Society because they do not know what it is, and the latter do not care to because they do not know the good it does. It is evident therefore that all men (since all men are born as infants) are born unfit for society; and very many (perhaps the majority) remain so throughout their lives, because of mental illness or lack of training [*disciplina*]. Yet as infants and as adults they do have a human nature. Therefore man is made fit for Society not by nature, but by training. Furthermore, even if man were born in a condition to desire society, it does not follow that he was born suitably equipped to enter society. Wanting is one thing, ability another. For even those who arrogantly reject the equal conditions without which society is not possible, still want it." Hirschman argues that a coherent reconstruction of Hobbes's views implies that, in the Hobbesian state of nature, there can be small associations, including matriarchal families (Hirschman 2016).

12 In the state of nature, "there are no Matrimoniall lawes" (Hobbes 2012, p. 310, ch. 20).

13 MECW, vol. 6, p. 506 [*Manifesto of the Communist Party*].

14 MECW, vol. 37, p. 807 [*Capital III*].

15 *History of Animals* 488a8; 589a3 (Aristotle 1965–1991); *Politics* 1253a7–18 (Aristotle 1932); 1278b15–30; *Nicomachean Ethics* 1097b8–1; 1162a16–19; 1169b16–22 (Aristotle 1926); *Eudemian Ethics* 1242a22–4 (Aristotle 1935).

16 Some of the controversies are summarized in Knoll 2017; cf. Adamson and Rapp 2021.

17 *History of Animals* 487b33–488a14.

18 This account relies on Depew 1995. The common goal needs to be something beyond reproduction, otherwise sexually reproducing species would automatically count as political, which is something that Aristotle wants to avoid. For some additional complexities, see Lloyd 2013.

19 Aristotle seems to underestimate the extent to which some gregarious animals, just by staying close to each other, produce important goods, such as mutual protection.

20 *Politics* 1253a7–18. See also what Aristotle says about humans and speech in *History of Animals* and in *Problems* (Aristotle 2011).

21 *Politics* 1252b29–31; cf. also *Politics* 1333a16–1334b5 (and book 10 of the *Nicomachean Ethics*).

22 *Politics* 1252a1–10. Later in the text, Aristotle says that the *polis* is a "partnership of households and clans in living well, and its object is a full and independent life" (*Politics* 1280b33–35). On why Aristotle sees the *polis* (as opposed to other, more cosmopolitan forms of cooperation) as the most supreme form of human association, see Depew 2019; cf. Chappell 2009.

23 *Politics* 1252b29–1253a4. Various questions can be asked about how the claims that Aristotle makes in this context (on the naturalness of the *polis*, on humans being more political than other animals, on the teleological links between the *polis* and other forms of association, and so on) are related. Some of the complexities emerge in the medieval discussions and interpretations (cf. Toivanen 2021).

24 The claims about "the most supreme of all goods," as well as those about the good life, need to be read alongside what is said in the *Nicomachean Ethics*.

25 *Politics* 1253a10.

26 *Politics* 1253a30–40. Aristotle says that someone who is "by nature and not merely by fortune citiless" is "either low in the scale of humanity or above it [...] inasmuch as he resembles an isolated piece at draughts." Aristotle also links being "citiless" with being "heartless" and being "a lover of war" (*Politics* 1253a4–a8). He acknowledges that there are humans who lack or fail to develop the impulse to participate in *polis*-like forms of association, but these are humans who do not achieve the kind of perfection that can be found in fully developed humans.

27 Hobbes 1997, p. 71, 5.5; cf. also 5.6.

28 Hobbes 2012, pp. 258–60, ch. 17. Cf. also Hobbes 1997, pp. 71–2, 5.5; and chapter 19 in *Elements of Law* (in Hobbes 2017).

29 Hobbes "is simply Aristotle turned upside down" (Depew 2009, p. 406); cf. Sorrel 1999.

30 Capitalism can be seen as an improvement compared with previous forms of cooperation partly because it "melts into air" some of the precapitalist constraints on human free development (MECW, vol. 6, p. 487; MECW, vol. 28, p. 95; cf. the discussion on free individuality in MECW, vols. 28–29). The unidirectional view of changes in human cooperation that Marx advocates in the *Manifesto* is replaced by a more nuanced and multidimensional account in his later reflections; see Anderson 2010; Musto 2016.

31 MECW, vol. 6, p. 506 [*Manifesto*], MECW, vol. 35, p. 588 [*Capital I*], MECW, vol. 37, p. 807 [*Capital III*], MECW, vol. 24, p. 87 [*Critique of the Gotha Programme*]; see also MECW, vol. 5, pp. 50–3 [*German Ideology*].

32 Within a Marxian account, there is room for the view that historical forces (as opposed to internal drives) might push us in the direction of better forms of cooperation. In various works, Marx controversially suggests that there are tendencies leading human societies toward communism; see for example the oft-cited claim, in the *Manifesto*, that "what the bourgeoisie [...] produces, above all, is its own grave diggers" (MECW, vol. 6, p. 496). There are ways of interpreting claims like these that avoid deterministic and teleological conceptions of history. One could even argue that Marx and Engels's teleological-sounding claims are nothing but performatives. It is worth remembering that, immediately after having read his copy of the first edition of *On the Origin of Species*, Engels writes to Marx: "Darwin, by the way, whom I'm reading just now, is absolutely splendid. There was one aspect of teleology that had yet to be demolished, and that has now been done. Never before has so grandiose an attempt been made to demonstrate historical evolution in Nature, and certainly never to such good effect" (MECW, vol. 40, p. 551 [December 11 or 12, 1859]; Darwin's book was published on November 24, 1859).

33 In some of his early works, Marx argues that we are currently separated from "[our] *human* nature, [our] true nature, [our] communal nature" (MECW, vol. 3, p. 228 [*Comments on James Mill*]). The suggestion is that we are currently less than fully human as a result of our modes of life, and that the abolition of capitalism will make us fully human. On this view, being fully human consists in having specific modes of life, rather than in possessing specific intrinsic characters (such as certain rational faculties). In other contexts, Marx does not depict human nature as an ideal to be achieved (or fully actualized), or as a telos, but rather as something that we currently have and that, in all its positive and negative aspects, is continuously transformed by historical processes (MECW, vol. 6, p. 192; vol. 35, p. 187). There are various ways of making sense of (and perhaps reconciling) these two Marxian ways of thinking about human nature. It is in any case important to realize that Marx's claims about human nature being continuously transformed can be embraced without embracing his views on what social transformations are desirable and likely to occur. Moreover, his views on what changes are desirable and forthcoming can be formulated without using the language of human nature and without accepting a teleological notion of human nature. Marx never abandons the claim that capitalism separates us from the best possible forms of human cooperation; and it is interesting that, in the third volume of *Capital*, this claim is again expressed by using the language of human nature: in the "realm of freedom," says Marx we will have "conditions [...] most favourable to, and worthy of, [our] human nature" (MECW, vol. 37, p. 807).

34 MECW, vol. 35, pp. 187–8 [*Capital I*]. Compare this with what Marx writes in MECW, vol. 3, pp. 276–7 [*Economic and Philosophic Manuscripts of 1844*].

35 MECW, vol. 25, pp. 459–60 [*Dialectics of Nature*].

36 Engels also argues that tool production and tool use are present in non-human animals and cannot therefore explain the difference between human niche construction and animal niche construction: "Animals in the narrower sense also have tools, but only as limbs of their bodies: the ant, the bee, the beaver; animals also produce, but their productive effect on surrounding nature, in relation to nature, amounts to nothing at all. Man alone has succeeded in impressing his stamp on nature, not only by shifting plant and animal species from one place to another, but also by so altering the aspect and climate of his dwelling-place, and even the plants and animals themselves, that the consequences of his activity can disappear only with the general extinction of the terrestrial globe" (MECW, vol. 25, pp. 459–60 [*Dialectics of Nature*]). Engels is less of a discontinuist than Marx; but it should be stressed that there are passages where Engels uses discontinuist formulations. He claims, for instance, that humans "produce" whereas animals "garner"; that humans "master" the environment whereas animals "use" it; and that animals "have a history" ("their descent and gradual evolution"), and to some extent "take part in it," but they do not truly make their history, since their history is "made for them" (cf. MECW, vol. 45, p. 108; MECW, vol. 25, p. 460; MECW, vol. 25, pp. 330–1).

37 MECW, vol. 25, pp. 461–2. A slightly different (less niche-constructionist) formulation of the same idea can be found in MECW, vol. 25, pp. 330–1 [*Dialectics of Nature*].

38 Contemporary research indicates that the differences between human niche construction and the niche construction of other primates (our closest evolutionary relatives) are mainly due to the cumulative dynamics that human culture generates, and to the mechanisms (not only psychological) that favor such dynamics; cf. Henrich 2016; Laland 2017; Boyd and Richerson 2008; Sterelny 2012.

39 Engels writes: "Only conscious organisation of social production [...] can lift mankind above the rest of the animal world as regards the social aspect, in the same way that production in general has done this for mankind in the specifically biological aspect. Historical development makes such an organisation daily more indispensable, but also with every day more possible. From it will date a new epoch of history, in which mankind itself, and with mankind all branches of its activity, and particularly natural science, will experience an advance that will put everything preceding it in the deepest shade" (MECW, vol. 25, pp. 331 [*Dialectics of Nature*]). Engels also points out that the "regulation [of the effects of our world-transforming activities] requires something more than mere knowledge. It requires a complete revolution in our hitherto existing mode of production, and simultaneously a revolution in our whole contemporary social order" (MECW, vol. 25, pp. 462; cf. also MECW, vol. 5, pp. 51–2 [*German Ideology*]).

40 MECW, vol. 37, p. 807 [*Capital III*]; "interchange with Nature" translates "*Stoffwechsel mit der Natur*" [metabolic exchange with nature]; for the German text, see Marx and Engels 1956–1999 (*Werke*, MEW), bd. 25, p. 828. This passage needs to be compared with the passage, a few pages earlier, about how capitalism generates an "irreparable break [*unheilbaren Riß*]" in the socially mediated metabolic exchange between humans and the rest of nature (MECW, vol. 37, p. 807; p. 799; MEW bd. 25, p. 821). On the "kingdom of freedom" according to Engels, see MECW, vol. 24, p. 324 [*Socialism: Utopian and Scientific*], and vol. 25, p. 270 [*Anti-Dühring*]. In *Theories of Surplus Value*, Marx refers to "production for its own sake [which] means nothing but the development of human productive forces, in other words the *development of the richness of human nature as an end in itself*" (MECW, vol. 31, p. 347).

41 MECW, vol. 37, p. 807 [*Capital III*], translation modified ("*würdigsten und adäquatesten*," MEW bd. 25, p. 828); Benjamin 1969, p. 257.

42 Roes 1998, p. 8.

43 On *eusociality*, see Wilson 1971; Crespi and Yanega 1995. Cranes are not eusocial, but Aristotle was impressed by the flight formations of these birds and by how the leaders govern such formations through honking noises; cf. *History of Animals* 614bl8–27; cf. Depew 1995. The evolution of sterile workers is discussed in Darwin 1859, ch. 7.

44 The division of labor among different kinds of sterile workers can also be rigid, although in some species workers may change roles as they age.

45 Cf. Buss 1988; Maynar-Smith and Szathmàry 1998; Wilson and Hölldobler 2009; Moritz and Southwick 1992; Whitfield 2002; Forster and Ratnieks 2000; Helanterä and Ratnieks 2010.

46 Cf.: "In a higher phase of communist society, after the enslaving subordination of the individual to the division of labour [...] has vanished, [...] only then can [...] society inscribe on its banners: From each according to his abilities, to each according to his needs!" (MECW, vol. 24, p. 87 [*Critique of the Gotha Programme*]).

47 For an (incomplete) account of the ways in which bees have been used in political theorizing in Western thought across the centuries (including in discussions of socialist and communist societies), see Wilson 2007.

48 Cf. "Sartre once said that if humanity proved to be incapable of achieving communism—this was back when the word was used innocently, so to speak—then, after humanity dies out, it could be said that it had been of no more interest than ants" (Badiou 2019, p. 9). Alain Badiou contends that "The Other" is that "through which our commonality is realized as communism" and that "after the Neolithic Revolution, which created humanity as it still is today—resourceful and ingenious, master over nature and ubiquitous, but full of inequality and ferocious—will come, must come, the second revolution, the communist revolution" (p. 35).

Chapter 2

1 Rousseau 2012, p. 62, p. 66 [*Discourse on Inequality*]. Rousseau writes that "it is no light undertaking to disentangle what is original from what is artificial in the present nature of man, and to know correctly a state which no longer exists, which perhaps never did exist, which probably never will exist, and about which it is nevertheless necessary to have correct notions in order to judge our present state properly" (p. 52). On how to interpret the phrase "perhaps never did exist" in this passage, see Kelly 2006.

2 Rousseau 2012, p. 116.

3 Rousseau 2012, p. 69.

4 Rousseau 2012, p. 87. Cf. Baker 1998.

5 Rousseau uses the French words "*premier*," "*veritable*," and "*pur*" to qualify the state of nature; "relation" translates "*commerce*"; see Rousseau 2007.

6 Rousseau 2012, p. 76.

7 Rousseau 2012, p. 128 and p. 141. Would Hobbes agree that entirely nonlinguistic humans, if they could exist, would be peaceful? Possibly (cf. Pettit 2008).

8 Rousseau 2012, p. 127, p. 82.

9 Rousseau 2012, pp. 96–7. In the state of nature there is no "pride" and therefore "neither hatred nor a desire for vengeance" (p. 147). Rousseau considers "pity" a "natural virtue": one that is "so natural that the beasts themselves sometimes show perceptible signs of it" (p. 83). In humans, this virtue becomes important when we abandon solitary modes of life and start living together.

10 Rousseau 2012, p. 117. Also: "The human soul altered in the bosom of society" (p. 51). Rousseau 1990, p. 213: "Human nature does not go backward, and it is never possible to return to the times of innocence and equality once they have been left behind."

11 Rousseau 2012, pp. 71–2 [*Discourse on Inequality*].

12 Rousseau writes: "The example of savages, almost all of whom are found at this point, seems to confirm that the human race was made to remain in it forever, that this state is the veritable youth of the world, and that all subsequent progress has been in appearance so many steps toward the perfection of the individual, and in fact toward the decrepitude of the species" (Rousseau 2012, p. 97). For a discussion of the initial stages of civilization, see also the *Essay on the Origins of Language* (Rousseau 2009).

13 Rousseau 2012 [*Discourse on Inequality*], Note X. On the role of orangutans in Rousseau's thinking about the "pure state of nature," and on his disagreement with Buffon, see the discussion in Wokler 2001, ch. 3; see also Wokler 1978; Moron 1995; Cribb et al. 2014.

14 Rousseau 2012, p. 115.

15 Cf. MECW, vol. 5, p. 5.

16 On Hobbes's political motivations, see Hamilton 2009. Some of Rousseau's motivations are discussed in Wokler 2001.

17 "Everything is good when it springs from the hands of our Creator; everything degenerates when shaped by the hands of man" (Rousseau 1979, p. 37).

18 Gen. 2:17. Scripture quotations are from the New Revised Standard Version Updated Edition, copyright © 2021 by the National Council of Churches of Christ in the U.S.A.; used by permission.

19 Gen. 2:18.

20 Gen. 3:1–6.

21 Gen. 3:16. It is only after this change in social relations that Adam gives a name to the "woman" and calls her Eve, Gen. 3:20.

22 Gen. 3:16.

23 Gen. 3:17–19.

24 Gen. 3:7.

25 Gen. 3:10.

26 Gen. 2:17.

27 Gen. 3:19.

28 Gen. 3:22.

29 Cf. Schmid 2008; we are told in Gen 5:5 that Adam dies at the age of 930.

30 Smith 2019, p. 37. Smith also reports Igal German's claim that the use of the term "Fall" to refer to Adam's expulsion from Eden comes from Methodius (260–311CE).

31 Rom 5:12. Paul is famously proposing a parallel between Adam and Christ; cf. 1Cor. 15:21-22. As is well known, these are some of the most debated parts of the New Testament.

32 Augustine 1998, 13.14. On Augustine's argument in support of the claim that all sinned in Adam, see Agamben 2020. For the thesis that we "all died in Adam," see Augustine 1998, 13.23, 14.1.

33 Augustine 1998, 13.23; cf. also 14.6, 14.11. In 14.12, Augustine explains "why other sins do not change human nature in the way it was changed by the transgressions of the first two human beings."

34 *De nuptiis et concupiscentia,* ch. 7; translation from Schaff 1887, p. 266. Later in the same work, Augustine writes: "Even the liquid contained in the urinary vessels obeys the command to flow from us at our pleasure, and when we are not pressed with its overflow; while the vessels, also, which contain the liquid, discharge without difficulty, if they are in a healthy state, the office assigned them by our will of propelling, pressing out, and ejecting their contents. With how much greater ease and quietness, then, if the generative organs of our body were compliant, would natural motion ensue, and human conception be effected" (ch. 53; p. 305).

35 "The soul is ashamed of the body's resistance to it" (Augustine 1998, 14.23); "The reproductive members [...] are called *pudenda* because lust has greater power to move them than reason," *Contra Iulianum* IV, 5.35; translation from Augustine 1957.

36 Augustine 1998, 13.13, 13.15, 14.16, 14.17, 14.18, 14:19, 14.23, 14:26; cf. Agamben 2010.

37 Augustine 1998, 14.15.

38 Augustine 1998, 14.21; 14.23; 14:26.

39 *Contra Iulianum* IV, 4.24; Augustine 1957; cf. Gal. 5:17.

40 Cf. *De peccatorum meritis et remissione et de baptismo parvulorum* (translation in Schaff 1887).

41 Cova 2014.

42 Agamben 2020, p. 9; cf. also Sahlins 2008.

43 Cf. Lemetti 2011, p. 50.

44 Hobbes 1839–1845, vol. 5, pp. 367–8 [*Questions Concerning Liberty, Necessity, and Chance*]; Hobbes 1839–1845, vol. 4, pp. 273–4 [*Of Liberty and Necessity*]; cf. also Hobbes 1997, p. 111, 9.9. See the discussion in Pink 2016 and Pink (forthcoming). I would like to thank Tom Pink for allowing me to read and cite his manuscript.

45 Hobbes writes: "The truth is, that man is a creature of greater power than other living creatures are, but his advantages do consist especially in two things: whereof one is the use of speech, by which men communicate one with another, and join their forces together, and by which also they register their thoughts that they perish not, but be reserved, and afterwards joined with other thoughts, to produce general rules for the direction of their actions. There be beasts that see better, others that hear better, and others that exceed mankind in other senses. Man excelleth beasts only in making of rules to himself, that is to say, in remembering, and in reasoning aright upon that which he remembereth. They which do so, deserve an honour above brute beasts. But they which mistaking the use of words, deceive themselves and others, introducing error, and seducing men from the truth, are so much less to be honoured than brute beasts, as error is more vile than ignorance. So that it is not merely the nature of man, that makes him worthier than other Creatures, but the knowledge that he acquires by meditation, and by the right use of reason in making good rules of his future actions. The other advantage a man hath, is the use of his hands for the making of those things which are instrumental to his well-being. But this advantage is not a matter of so great honour, but that a man may speak negligently of it without offence" (Hobbes 1839–1845, vol. 5, pp. 186–7 [*Questions*]). On humans not being superior to animals, see also, for instance, Hobbes 2012, pp. 1166 [ch. 1 of the Appendix to the Latin *Leviathan*], as well as various remarks in *De Homine*. For an account of Hobbes's political views that focuses on what Hobbes says about language, see Pettit 2008.

46 Bramhall, in Hobbes 1839–1845, vol. 5, pp. 110–11. Bramhall also writes that from Hobbes's view "one of these two absurdities must needs follow: either that Adam did not sin, and that there is no such thing as sin in the world, because it proceeds naturally, necessarily, and essentially from God; or that God is more guilty of it, and more the cause of evil than man, because man is extrinsically, inevitably determined, but so is not God" (p. 111). See the discussion in Pink (forthcoming).

47 Hobbes 1839–1845, vol. 5, pp. 102; cf. Pink (forthcoming). Hobbes also writes: "*Doth God reprehend him [Adam] for doing that which he hath antecedently determined him that he must do?* I answer, no; but he convinceth and instructeth him, that though immortality was so easy to obtain, as it might be had for the abstinence from the fruit of one only tree, yet he could not obtain it but by pardon, and by the sacrifice of Jesus Christ: nor is there here any punishment, but only a reducing of Adam and Eve to their original mortality, where death was no punishment but a gift of God. In which mortality he lived near a thousand years, and had a numerous issue, and lived without misery, and I believe shall at the resurrection obtain the immortality which then he lost" (p. 103); see also vol. 4, pp. 246–7; for Bramhall's response, see Bramhall 1844, pp. 303–4 [*Castigations of Mr. Hobbes' Animadversions*]. Bramhall invokes the events of Eden to criticize various claims that Hobbes makes in *Leviathan*. According to Bramhall: "the Hobbian nature of man, is worse than the nature of Bears, or Wolves, or the most savage wild beasts" (Bramhall 1844, p. 551 [*Of Leviathan*]).

48 Hobbes 1839–1845, vol. 4, p. 353 [*Answer to Bishop Bramhall*]. Hobbes writes: "I understand […] that Adam could have lived for ever as a result of eating the fruit of the tree of life, and that he was created immortal not in his own nature, but only by virtue of the tree of life. I understand, further, that the punishment inflicted on Adam for violating the divine command was mortality, which followed necessarily from the fact that he had lost the thing without which he could not live for ever" (Hobbes 2012, p. 1162 [Appendix ch. 1]); cf. also pp. 698–700 [ch. 38] and pp. 1234–6 [Appendix ch. 3].

49 According to Bramhall, the human will (and the capacity not to sin) has been damaged by the events in the garden, but our will is still free, even in its postlapsarian state (Bramhall 1844, p. 234 [*Castigations*]). In some sections of his debate with Bramhall, Hobbes invokes John Calvin's hyper-Augustinian view, according to which the freedom of the will has not just been damaged but has been completely lost as a result of the Fall (Hobbes 1839–1845, vol. 5, p. 298 [*Questions*]). Hobbes uses Calvin's view in support of some of his claims, but for Hobbes the human will has always been unfree: we have always been animal-like in this respect. As Pink puts it, "any freedom of will that Calvin supposes us to have lost is supposed by Hobbes to be not lost but strictly unintelligible" (Pink 2016, p. 185); see also the discussion in Pink (forthcoming). For the Augustinian roots of Calvin's views on these matters, see Augustine 1998, 12.22, 13.23.

50 Augustine 1998, 14.10, 14.11.

51 Augustine also argues that the elect will have better bodies than Adam and Eve; cf. Augustine 1998, bk. 13 and bk. 22. Given that the Edenic events resulted in the loss of control over one's genitals, eternal life should bring back such control; see the comments in Agamben 2010.

52 Cf. Hobbes 1839–1845, vol. 4, p. 353 [*Answer to Bishop Bramhall*]; Hobbes 2012, Appendix ch. 1. As for those who will not be allowed into the Kingdom of God, see what Hobbes says in ch. 38 of *Leviathan* and Bramhall's critical comments (1844, p. 535, pp. 538–9 [*Castigations*]).

53 Hobbes 2012, p. 642, ch. 35; see also p. 764, ch. 41.

54 Cf. Hobbes 2012, ch. 43; see also Hobbes 2012, p. 764 [ch. 41], p. 960 [ch. 44].

55 Hobbes 2012, ch. 35 and ch. 38. See also how Hobbes summarizes his views on the Kingdom of God in chapter 44 of *Leviathan*: Hobbes 2012, p. 960.

56 Hobbes 2012, ch. 38 and ch. 44. This is how Hobbes interprets "My Kingdome is not of this World" (John 18:36) in Hobbes 2012, p. 726 [ch. 38] and the discussion in ch. 42. On the resurrection of bodies, see ch. 38 of *Leviathan* and ch. 1 of the Appendix (Hobbes 2012, pp. 1158–68).

57 In his comments on the opening words of *Leviathan*, Jacques Derrida (2009) emphasizes that, for Hobbes, the Leviathan (the "Artificial Animal") is an imitation of God. After the Last Judgment, this anthropogenic imitation will become useless. See Hobbes 2012, p. 16 [*Introduction*]: "NATURE (the Art whereby God hath made and governes the World) is by the Art of man, as in many other things, so in this also imitated, that it can make an Artificial Animal."

58 Hobbes 2012, p. 260, ch. 17.

59 In the frontispiece of the first edition of *Leviathan*, the Leviathan is represented as a colossus (see the discussion in Skinner 2009). The body of the colossus is composed of human bodies. These bodies, which are miniscule relative to the giant as a whole, are absent in the head, which instead is the giant head of the (one and only) monarch. All the tiny humans are looking toward the giant head. Giorgio Agamben argues that the way the Leviathan is depicted in this frontispiece "derives directly from the Pauline conception, present in various passages of the Letters, according to which Christ is the head (*kephalē*) of the *ekklēsia*, that is, of the assembly of the faithful" (Agamben 2017, p. 286 [*Stasis: Civil War as a Political Paradigm*]). Likewise from the Pauline letters, according to Agamben's reading, derives the idea that Christ will render human political power inoperative.

60 Agamben writes: "Common-wealth and state of nature do not coincide, but are conjoined in a complicated relation. The state of nature, as Hobbes explains in the preface to *De Cive*, is what appears when one considers the city as if it were dissolved (*civitas […] tanquam dissoluta consideretur […] ut qualis sit natura humana […] recte intelligatur*), which is to say, from the perspective of civil war. In other words, the state of nature is a mythological projection into the past of civil war; conversely, civil war is a projection of the state of nature into the city: it is what appears when one considers the city from the perspective of the state of nature" (Agamben 2017, pp. 281–2 [*Stasis*]; see also *Homo Sacer*).

61 According to Hobbes, the Kingdom of God does not coincide with "the present Church" (Hobbes 2012, p. 960, ch. 44); the Pope has no "Power without his own Dominions" (p. 870, ch. 42) and he has no "Jurisdiction in the Dominion of any other Prince" (p. 908, ch. 42). There is no "universall Monarchy" with the Pope as its "Univerall King" (ch. 47). Here, Hobbes's immediate practical aims emerge.

62 Morgan 1877, p. 552; cf. Marx 1974, p. 137; MECW, vol. 24, p. 350 [*Drafts of the Letter to Vera Zasulich*]; MECW, vol. 26, p. 276 [*Origin of the Family, Private Property and the State*]. Brief discussions of "ancient," "communal," or "tribal" modes of life can be found in *The German Ideology*, the *Economic Manuscripts of 1857–58*, and *Capital*. One of the reasons why Marx and Engels found Morgan's work interesting was that it offered them a way to elaborate ideas about small-scale communism that they had been exploring since 1846 (cf. MECW, vol. 24, vol. 26, vol. 27).

63 Cf. MECW, vol. 26, p. 272 [*Origin of the Family, Private Property and the State*]; MECW, vol. 25, p. 268 [*Anti-Dühring*].

Chapter 3

1 *Politics* 1260a7–14.

2 On barbarians as natural slaves, see *Politics* 1252b5ff, 1259a29ff; on the ferocious behaviors of barbarians, see *Politics* 1138b19, *Nicomachean Ethics* 1145a31; 1148b19ff; *Parts of Animals* 673a25; on the inferior mental abilities of barbarians, see *History of Animals* 668b1; *Problems* 910b24–29; 911a3.

3 *Politics* 1253b; *Nicomachean Ethics* 1161a–b. It is worth noting that Hobbes criticizes Aristotle's ideas on natural slavery (Hobbes 1997, 3.17; Hobbes 2012, ch. 15); Rousseau discusses slavery in *The Social Contract* (Rousseau 2012).

4 *Politics* 1280a32–35: "the polis was formed not for the sake of life only but rather for the good life (for otherwise a collection of slaves or of lower animals would be a *polis*, but as it is, it is not a *polis*, because slaves and animals have no share in happiness or in living according to rational choice)." Barbarians, at least in general, "have no class of natural rulers," which also means that in barbarian societies slaves and women have the same "rank": in those societies "the conjugal partnership is a partnership of female slave and male slave" (*Politics* 1252b6–9). Cf. also: *Nicomachean Ethics* 1095a17–22; 1142b34ff.

5 See, for example, Lienemann 2021. Aristotle contends that some ethnic groups are physiologically inferior to others and women are physiologically inferior to men. On the links and tensions between Aristotle's physiological and political/ethical views, see Cagnoli Fiecconi 2021.

6 Cf. Karbowski 2019. Aristotle suggests that a well-functioning human community needs, among its members, individuals who are by nature inferior: "Thus the female and the slave are by nature distinct (for nature makes nothing as the cutlers make the Delphic knife, in a niggardly way, but one thing for one purpose; for so each tool will be turned out in the finest perfection, if it serves not many uses but one)" (*Politics* 1252b1–5). On hierarchies, see *Politics* 1254a22–33.

7 Cf. Vegetti and Ademollo 2016.

8 On the events that led to the Valladolid debate, on how the debate unfolded, and on its significance, see Hanke 1959; Pagden 1982.

9 Sepúlveda was not the first to invoke the Aristotelian idea of natural slavery in relation to non-Western populations. In 1519, the Scottish theologian John Mair wrote: "These people [the inhabitants of the Antilles] live like

beasts on either side of the equator; and beneath the poles there are wild men as Ptolemy says in his *Tetrabiblos*. And this has now been demonstrated by experience, wherefore the first person to conquer them, justly rules over them because they are by nature slaves. As the Philosopher says [...], it is clear that some men are by nature slaves, others by nature free [...]. And it is just that one man should be a slave and another free, and it is fitting that one man should rule and another obey [...]. On this account the Philosopher says [...] that this is the reason why the Greeks should be masters over the barbarians because, by nature, the barbarians and slaves are the same"; quoted in Pagden 1982, pp. 38–9; see also the quote from a text by Spanish jurist Juan de Matienzo (p. 41).

10 Quoted in Hanke 1959, p. 47.

11 Quoted in Hanke 1959, p. 47.

12 Quoted in Stuurman 2017, p. 225.

13 Hanke 1951, p. 61; cf. also the discussion in Pagden 1982 and Stuurman 2017.

14 Quoted in Stuurman 2017, p. 227.

15 Las Casas, *Apologética historia summaria de las gentes destas Indias*, pp. 127–8; quoted in Hanke 1959, p. 112. In a first phase of his polemic against those who used Aristotelian ideas to justify the enslavement and exploitation of the Indigenous populations, Las Casas claimed that Aristotle was a "gentile burning in hell whose doctrine should be accepted only so far as it conformed to Christian thought" (quoted in Hanke 1951, p. 69). In later works (such as the *Apologética*), he changed tack and argued that the Indigenous met the Aristotelian requirements for full rationality.

16 Las Casas, *Historia de las Indias*, I, prólogo; quoted in Hanke 1959, p. 113.

17 See the quote from Las Casas's *Apologética* in Wynter 2003, p. 284.

18 According to Wynter, the "manifesto" of such a view is Pico della Mirandola's *De hominis dignitate*: "Pico rewrote the Judeo-Christian origin narrative of Genesis. Adam, rather than having been placed in the Garden of Eden, then having fallen, then having been expelled with Eve from the garden by God, is shown by Pico to have not fallen at all. Instead, he had come into existence when God, having completed his Creation and wanting someone to admire His works, had created Man on a model unique to him, then placed him at the center/midpoint of the hierarchy of this creation, commanding him to 'make of himself' what he willed to be—to decide for himself whether to fall to the level of the beasts by giving into his passions, or, through the use of his reason, to rise to the level of the angels" (Wynter 2003, pp. 276–7). Pico wrote his work in 1486, just a few years before Christopher Columbus's arrival in the Americas.

19 According to Wynter (2003), the discourses about rationality and race (and therefore racialization) became biologized in the nineteenth century.

Chapter 4

1 General ways of thinking about human nature can be called "concepts," "notions," or "conceptions" of human nature. For our purposes, it does not matter which of these three terms is chosen. All of them appear in the literature.

2 There is no need in this context to provide precise criteria for distinguishing sciences routinely classified as "natural" from other sciences. All I am doing here is rejecting what I take to be implausible attempts to insulate concepts of human nature from programs of inquiry that, for various psycho-historical reasons, have acquired the label of "natural sciences." Two things need to be said. First, there are obviously important issues about the status of the natural sciences and about the correct ways of relating these sciences to human praxis. Many debates on (the various ways of understanding) *naturalism* are, directly or indirectly, about this. Second, I acknowledge that those who, with Heidegger, radically reject "zoological" ways of thinking about the human will be unsatisfied (cf. Heidegger 2014, p. 158; see also the discussion on "*humanitas*" and "*animalitas*," the critique of "biologism," and the refusal to "locate man within being as one being among others" in the "Letter on humanism," Heidegger 1977). Heidegger, writes Agamben (2003, p. 39), is "the philosopher of the twentieth century who more than any other strove to separate man from the living being." I will not discuss the Heideggerian perspective (and its variations, including the one found in Arendt 1958).

3 The channel-of-communication metaphor appears in a useful comment made by Cecilia Heyes: "If the concept of human nature is eliminated from scientific discourse, it will almost certainly continue to be used 'out in the world', but that usage will not be informed or constrained by science; an important channel of communication between science and the public will close down. For this reason, and because the concept of human nature plays an important role in defining explanatory projects within science [...], I believe it should be patched up rather than eliminated" (Heyes 2018a, p. 76; cf. also Godfrey-Smith 2014, p. 139). My use of the metaphor differs from Heyes's, since I want my version to be more general and to focus on the links between ideas about human nature and human praxis (and only indirectly on what happens or should happen within specific research programs in science). The channel-of-communication metaphor, in its general version, is one possible way of dealing with the "normative" dimensions or implications of the language of human nature. Many accounts of the concept of human nature (including Heyes's) fail to properly address these dimensions; but there are accounts that emphasize such dimensions. For example, Christopher Berry (1986) argues that the concept of human nature is a "practical concept," both "descriptive" and "prescriptive"; and Martha Nussbaum (1992; 1995) claims that an account of human nature is inherently ethical. Neither Berry nor Nussbaum, in my view, provides a satisfactory account, but they both address important issues often neglected in theories that focus on the use of the concept of human nature within scientific discourse.

4 Hull 1994, p. 313; cf. Okasha 2002.

5 Darwin 1851a; 1851b; 1854a; 1854b.

6 Darwin 1854a, p. 155.

7 Darwin 1854a, p. 1.

8 In his autobiography, while describing his childhood, Darwin writes: "The passion for collecting which leads a man to be a systematic naturalist, a virtuoso, or a miser, was very strong in me, and was clearly innate, as none of my sisters or brother ever had this taste" (Darwin 1887, vol. 1, p. 28).

9 Darwin 1868.

10 Sterelny 2018, p. 108. The ubiquity of variation plays an important role in the Modern Evolutionary Synthesis, but it is also an important element within the Extended Evolutionary Synthesis, which deals with aspects of the evolutionary process that the Modern Synthesis is unable to explain satisfactorily (cf. West-Eberhard 2003; Laland et al. 2014).

11 Darwin 1859; 1868; 1871.

12 We can use the term "Darwinian selection" to refer to all selection processes that influence the frequencies of cross-generationally stable variants, including selection dynamics that are different from those that Darwin described. See Godfrey-Smith 2009 for a general account of Darwinian populations and selection processes.

13 Cf. Sterelny and Griffiths (1999): "ubiquity of variation" (p.10).

14 Cf. Desmond and Moore 1992.

15 Hull 1986, p. 11: "Perhaps a unimodal distribution of characters might be found which succeeds in placing all human beings in a single species and in keeping all non-humans out. If so, this [...] would be an evolutionary happenstance and might well change in time." Cf. the discussion of essentialism in Dennett 1995.

16 Cf. Godfrey-Smith and Sterelny 2016.

17 Genetic encoding is one way to make sense of the (pre-theoretic) notion of innateness. On this notion and the links connecting lack of learning, genetic evolution, developmental robustness, and related properties, see Mameli and Bateson 2006; 2011; Bateson 1991; Mameli 2008. It is worth noting that innate traits do not need to be present in all members of the species, and they do not even need to be species-typical; on a standard understanding of the term, some of Darwin's innate traits might be different from the innate traits of his siblings.

18 In current humans, there is less genetic variation than one would expect on the basis of comparisons with other primates (Kaessmann et al. 2001; cf. Bergström et al. 2020). This is a contingent fact, likely the result of one or more recent evolutionary bottlenecks in our lineage.

19 Sterelny and Griffiths 1999, p. 186.

20 Proponents of ideal-type essentialism need not believe that variation in phenotypic and genetic traits is "illusory" (cf. Mayr 1959). However, they can maintain that such variation can be ignored when discussing the human essence. For a discussion of population thinking in relation to essentialism, see Sober 1980.

21 The view that variation, as a property of populations, is crucial in evolutionary dynamics is compatible with the view that developmental and ecological constraints on the generation of transmissible variation can play important roles in evolutionary processes.

22 It should also be noted that what is selectively advantageous relative to one kind of selection dynamic might be selectively disadvantageous relative to a different kind of selection. For example, Darwin argues that the peacock's tail is due to the sexual selection generated by the aesthetic preferences of peahens (Darwin 1859, p. 89; Darwin 1871). Being so shiny and big, the tail is disadvantageous in terms of natural selection, because it makes the peacock more vulnerable to predation attacks, but it is advantageous in terms of sexual selection, due to peahens' sexual preferences. Richard Prum (2017) argues that some human behavioral traits might have been affected by sexual selection in similar ways.

23 Cf. Solinas 2015. This claim is compatible with the so-called "teleological" theory of the function of biological body parts and processes, at least if that theory is understood in deflationary terms; for a discussion that focuses on Darwin, see Lennox 1993; on the teleological theory of biological function, see Godfrey-Smith 2014, ch. 4.

24 Facts about fitness differences, selection processes, or developmental outcomes are sometimes expressed by means of metaphorical *ought* statements. Some biologists might say that humans ought to have certain traits. They might mean that humans with those traits tend to do better than conspecifics in terms of survival and reproduction (in some specific circumstances); or they might mean that most humans, possibly as a result of past selection processes, have genes that reliably lead to the development of those traits (in some specific circumstances). In any case, facts about fitness differences, selection dynamics, and developmental outcomes do not dictate how humans ought to be.

25 B:232 in Darwin 1837–1838. Darwin writes that the "tree of life" can also be called the "coral of life" (B:25). On the "total shape of life on earth" and on why only some fragments of it can be considered tree-like, see Godfrey-Smith 2016, ch. 7.

26 Darwin 1843; Darwin 1859, p. 420.

27 Cf. Griffiths 1999; Okasha 2002; Godfrey-Smith 2014, p. 117: "Perhaps the essence of a species is its position in the tree of life." How exactly one should characterize the bio-genealogical relations in virtue of which an organism is a member of a given species is a complex issue. It can just be noted that, by giving us new ways to create beings genealogically related to us, biomedical, digital, and robotic technologies could make this issue even more complex.

28 On folk essentialism, see Atran et al. 1997; Gelman 2004; Haslam 2017.

29 The phrase "corporeal and mental endowments" is from Darwin 1859, p. 489.

30 Can the argument for not equating human nature with a bio-genealogical property be extended to other animal species and their natures? Ideas about the nature of dogs can have an impact on dogs' futures, and the same, *mutatis mutandis*, applies to other species. This is a reason to avoid equating the natures of non-human species with bio-genealogical properties. However, it should be noted that it is only via human thoughts and actions that ideas about dogs influence the modes of life of members of the species *Canis lupus familiaris*. Humans have a participant perspective in debates about human nature and human futures, while dogs do not have a similar perspective in debates about dogs' nature and dogs' futures. The participant perspective confers special significance to the human concept of human nature.

31 It is also worth saying that this way of thinking about human nature can serve as a communication channel between, on the one hand, *some* theological views about what we fundamentally are and, on the other, conversations about our modes of life. However, given its reference to immaterial (supernatural) entities, this way of thinking about human nature cannot serve as a communication channel between standard, mundane science and those conversations.

32 In principle, someone who advocates this view could concede that biology (via bio-genealogical considerations) can tell us who is human and who is not, while insisting that only normative reflection can tell us what it takes to be fully human.

33 Nussbaum writes: "to find out what our nature is seems to be one and the same thing as to find out what we deeply believe to be most important and indispensable. [...] Human nature cannot, and need not, be validated from the outside, because human nature just *is* an inside [evaluative] perspective" (Nussbaum 1995, pp. 106–21). Nussbaum attributes this view to Aristotle, due to the Aristotelian suggestion that human nature can be grasped by focusing on humans at their best (where this "best" is determined from an ethical and political standpoint). Nussbaum's "inside perspective" seems to me less preferable than a communication-channel approach. The communication-channel approach provides a better way of "rationally regulating" the interactions between our ideas about what we fundamentally are and human praxis, scientific research included. For a discussion of other contemporary Aristotle-inspired accounts, see Roughley 2021.

34 For the use of the term "superstition" in this context, cf. Ghiselin 1997, p. 1. There are many aspects of the debates on biological species essentialism that cannot be explored here. In the literature, one can find bio-genealogical accounts, property-clusters accounts (including accounts arguing that species have an essence that is at least partly constituted by clusters of genetic traits), as well as critiques of such accounts and of any attempt to retain essence talk in relation to biological species (cf. Boyd 1999; Wilson 1999; Griffiths 1999; Okasha 2002; Devitt 2008; 2010; 2021; Ereshefsky and Matthen 2005; Ereshefsky 2010; Walsh 2006; 2021; Lewens 2012b; Godman et al. 2020; Godman and Papineau 2020). Property-cluster accounts can arguably be classified as instances of the statistical-typicality view (see the discussion in the next chapter); other types of essentialist accounts—even assuming they can work from a biological viewpoint—are in any case unable to provide a satisfactory bridge between ideas about what we fundamentally are and conversations about our modes of life.

35 Skepticism about the language of human nature can be found in Levins and Lewontin 1985 (ch. 13); Hull 1986; Sterelny 2018; Kronfeldner (2016; 2018a; 2018b).

36 There is currently much discussion about conceptual engineering and its constraints (cf. Burgess et al. 2020; Chalmers 2020; Thomasson 2021; Machery 2021; Isaac and Koch 2022). While I will not delve into this debate here, it is important to note that proper attention needs to be given to the varied goals that might motivate us to critique (and find alternatives to) existing ways of thinking. Often, the discourse on this topic tends to be excessively narrow.

Chapter 5

1 "If by 'human nature' all one means is a trait which happens to be prevalent and important for the moment, then human nature surely exists" (Hull 1986, p. 9). This comment by David Hull is the starting point of debates about the statistical-typicality concept. The focus is on what is statistically typical in humans who are alive today ("for the moment") rather than in all species members (present, past, and future). This is due to the way the statistical-typicality concept interacts with the Darwinian transmutation of species. If species change in contingent ways, what is statistically typical now might be very different from what was statistically typical in the past and from what will be statistically typical in the future. (It should be noted that the term "species-typical" can be used, and is often used, to refer to traits that are statistically typical in the current members of the species, regardless of the reasons behind their statistical typicality. However, the term can also be used in other ways, which I will not consider here.)

2 Cf. Bateson 1991; Lewontin 2000; Kitcher 2001.

3 Mameli 2005.

4 Heyes writes: "We humans have created not just physical machines—such as pulleys, traps, carts, and internal combustion engines—but also mental machines; mechanisms of thought, embodied in our nervous systems, that enable our minds to go further, faster, and in different directions than the minds of any other animals. These distinctively human cognitive mechanisms include causal understanding, episodic memory, imitation, mindreading, normative thinking, and many more. They are 'gadgets', rather than 'instincts' (Pinker 1994), because, like many physical devices, they are products of cultural rather than genetic evolution" (Heyes 2018b, p. 1); cf. also Heyes 2018a; on cognitive instincts, see Pinker 1997; on the construction of human learning environments and their role in developmental processes, see Sterelny 2012; Tomasello 2019.

5 Heyes 2018a; 2018b.

6 Similarly, immunity against certain pathogens reemerges reliably across generations through reliable interactions with the relevant pathogens, traits influenced by the microbiota reemerge through reliable interactions with the relevant microorganisms, and so on.

7 Edouard Machery writes: "Human nature is the set of properties that humans tend to possess as a result of the evolution of their species. [...] This new account combines two proposals: the 'universality proposal' and the 'evolution proposal'. According to the former, traits that belong to human nature must be [statistically] typical of human beings; according to the latter, they must have evolved [through changes in gene frequencies]" (Machery 2018, p. 18; see also Machery 2008; 2012; 2016).

8 Cf. Lehrman 1970; Mameli and Bateson 2006; 2011; for a general discussion of the evolution of traits whose development involves "condition sensitivity," see West-Eberhard 2003. A trait whose development requires some forms of learning might evolve into a trait whose development requires different forms of learning, or into a trait whose development requires no learning; the evolutionary trajectory depends on the fitness costs and benefits of the available developmental options.

9 Machery's account can be seen as a rational reconstruction of the way of thinking about human nature found in the kind of "evolutionary psychology" elaborated by John Tooby and Leda Cosmides. They characterize human nature in terms of a genetically evolved "psychic unity" of the human species. This "unity" consists of a rich set of (statistically typical and domain-specific) cognitive modules, whose

development does not involve learning; see Barkow et al. 1992 and Pinker 1997; Pinker 2002. For a critique of this brand of evolutionary psychology, see Sterelny and Griffiths 1999; Buller 2005; Sterelny 2012; Heyes 2018a. Cosmides and Tooby's view can be compared with E.O. Wilson's. Wilson is more willing to discuss within-species evolved variation (as components of human nature) than are Cosmides and Tooby (Wilson 1975; 1978). Wilson has been criticized for his discussions of evolved genetic differences (see the articles in Caplan 1978; Lewontin et al. 1984). Presumably, it is to avoid similar attacks that Cosmides and Tooby focus mainly on species-typical traits.

10 In his exchange with Michel Foucault, Noam Chomsky says: "This schematism that makes it possible [for statistically typical human children] to derive complex and intricate [linguistic] knowledge on the basis of very partial [linguistic] data, is one fundamental component of human nature. [...] I assume that in other domains of human intelligence, in other domains of human cognition and behavior, something of the same sort must be true. Well, this mass of schematisms, innate organizing principles, which guides our social and intellectual and individual behavior, that is what I mean to refer to by the concept of human nature" (Chomsky and Foucault 1974, pp. 137–8; see also Chomsky 1959; Spelke et al. 1992).

11 Some accounts of human nature are presented as "essentialist" but, within the framework of my discussion, are best classified as post-essentialist since they appeal to statistical typicality rather than invariance or ideal typicality. The "causal essentialism" of Samuels (2012) is a case in point. On Samuels's account, the human essence is a set of statistically typical structures and mechanisms that proximally explain human psychological regularities. Samuels claims that the causal essence of a kind need not be something that individuates the kind; the human essence need not be definitional of being human, or of being fully human for that matter.

12 Akino et al. 2004.

13 Munoz-Arroyo et al. 2019; Godwin 2010. Mechanisms of adaptive plasticity need not be species-typical.

14 Phenotypic plasticity is not an epiphenomenal icing on the evolutionary cake. This is true for phenotypic plasticity in general (cf. West-Eberhard 2003) and for human cultural plasticity in particular (cf. Boyd and Richerson 2008; Sterelny 2012; Henrich 2016; Laland 2017).

15 The term "balancing selection" is often used to refer to selection processes that favor more than one variant (cf. Maynard-Smith 1998).

16 Wiley 2018.

17 Jablonski 2018.

18 Maynard-Smith 1982; Trivers 2002; Sober and Wilson 1997.

19 An interesting case is found in side-blotched lizards (*Uta stansburiana*). In this species, males have three different mating strategies. Orange-throat males are very aggressive and have large territories; blue-throat males are less aggressive and defend smaller territories; yellow-throat males do not have territories, but instead "sneak in" on females that already have a partner (receptive females also have yellow throats). The three strategies persist through a "rock-paper-scissors" dynamic. Because of the larger territories, orange-throat males can potentially attract more females than the blue-throat ones. But orange-throat males are more vulnerable to the sneaking attacks of yellow-throat males than are blue-throat males, who have better guarded territories. Orange beats blue, blue beats yellow, and yellow beats orange. These strategies are underpinned by different genetic variants: Sinervo and Lively 1996.

20 Kathryn Paige Harden writes: "the propaganda [of hereditarian pessimists] is this: if genetic differences between people cause differences in their life outcomes, then social change will be possible only by editing people's genes, not by changing the social world. [...] This hereditarian pessimism [...] is based on a fundamental misunderstanding of the relationship between genetic causes and environmental interventions. [...] The existence of genetic causes of social inequalities does not imply any hard boundaries on the possibility of change" (Harden 2021, p. 154, pp. 172–4).

21 The structure of these social conflicts can be inferred from debates on biomedical enhancement (Fukuyama 2002; Habermas 2003; Sandel 2008; Savulescu and Bostrom 2009; Harris 2010; Buchanan 2011), on disability (Buchanan et al. 2001; Garland-Thomson 2012; 2015; Sparrow 2015; Barnes 2015), on feminist approaches to technology (Firestone 1970; Haraway 1990; 2016; Mies and Shiva 1993; Hester 2018), on the Anthropocene (Moore 2016; Ellis 2018; Foster 2022; Saito 2023), and on "accelerationism," "transhumanism," "new materialism," "posthumanism" (More and Vita-More 2013; Ferrando 2013; Mackay and Avanessian 2014; Braidotti and Hlavajova 2018; Coccia 2020; Fluss and Frim 2022; Levidow and Pellizzoni 2022; Newman 2022).

22 It should be mentioned that worker bees have ovaries, although the queen blocks their development through chemical signals. Gonadal sex includes cases of blocked gonadal development as well as cases where aging gonads have stopped producing gametes.

23 The shape and structure of female genitals can generate selection pressures acting on the structure of male genitals, and vice versa; there can also be genital arms races (Prum 2017).

24 The internal incubation of fertilized eggs has been observed in male seahorses (Dudley et al. 2021).

25 Cf. Lloyd 2005; de Waal 2022.

26 This is the case in many bird species (cf. Prum 2017).

27 See Hrdy 2009.

28 Comparative and evolutionary approaches show that some human corporeal sex differences—such as those concerning body size and craniofacial features—have diminished over time; cf. Plavcan 2012.

29 Cf. Fausto-Sterling 2000; 2012.

30 Judith Butler (1990; 1993) insists on the performativity of gender and is critical of biological accounts. However, gender roles and their performativity can be integrated within a Darwinian framework: socially constructed gender roles are one important developmental resource among others. Fracchia (2022) offers a critique of approaches like Butler's, which theorize the body as a *tabula rasa*.

31 Labels such as "man" and "woman" play an important role in the web of social conflicts. When we discuss what to do with these labels, we are discussing human futures and making proposals about human modes of life. Biological theorizing per se cannot prescribe how one should link these labels to chromosomes, gonads, and genitals. Biology does not tell you whether you should use "man" to mean "XY human with two testes and a penis" or whether the term should be used in ways that track gender roles, self-identification, or other phenotypic features. Similarly, biology cannot dictate whether or not "woman" should be used to mean "XX human with ovaries, uterus, and vagina." How we use these labels is a political issue, beyond the scope of biological theory alone.

32 One form of balancing selection worth mentioning is heterozygous advantage, which has been suggested as an explanation for sickle-cell anemia and other pathological conditions.

33 This claim is, among other things, a rejection of the view that the language of human nature is inevitably exclusionary and dehumanizing (cf. Kronfeldner 2016; 2018a; 2018b; on dehumanization, and infrahumanization, cf. Haslam and Loughnan 2014). Essentializing tendencies can create problems, but the language of human nature is a tool that we can harness.

34 With regard to some patterns of variation, not all variants are perceived as equally worthy of attention. Wynter (2003) uses the term "overrepresentation" to refer to the phenomenon that occurs when a socially dominant way of being human is employed as an undisputed and unproblematic representation of "the human"—that is, as a representation of humans in general. "Man" and male-correlated traits are often used as proxies for humans in general; "people" are often represented as "white." These two examples concern traits (maleness and whiteness) that are not statistically typical, but a variant that "overrepresents itself" can also be a statistically typical one, as in the case of a neurotypical preference or ability that is taken to be *the way* humans are. Cf. Wynter 2001; McKittrick 2015; consider also: Simone de Beauvoir's thesis that "man" is the default or primary sex, while "woman" is "the second sex," and Frantz Fanon's realization that in France he was not perceived as fully human due to his skin color (Fanon 1967, ch. 5; Beauvoir 2009; cf. Wynter 2001; McKittrick 2015).

35 I am not the only one to point out that a post-essentialist concept of human nature should make room for important dimensions of human diversity: see Griffiths 2011; Ramsey 2013; 2018; Dupré 2015; Laland and Brown 2018. Karola Stotz and Paul Griffiths write: "If the human species is polymorphic, then this is part of the nature of the human species, something we should seek to understand when studying human beings as a kind. Many organisms also exhibit some form of phenotypic plasticity, the evolved ability to respond with different phenotypes to different environments. [...] This too is an important part of the nature of the species in question. [...] A concept of human nature [...] should accommodate the fact that humans are diverse and plastic" (Stotz and Griffiths 2018, p. 63; cf. Griffiths 2011, p. 328). However, standard arguments for a diversity-inclusive concept of human nature are incomplete because they overlook one crucial issue. If the concept of human nature did not play a general role in conversations about human futures, determining whether human-nature talk should be used exclusively in relation to statistically typical traits would be a terminological issue to be resolved within the life sciences. It is only in the context of a praxis-oriented philosophical reflection that we can come to see that our ways of thinking about human nature—our ways of using human-nature talk—have consequences beyond the life sciences, and that such consequences give us reasons to make room for diversity.

36 Heyes proposes an account of human nature that combines Machery's and Samuels's accounts. Both Machery and Samuels regard statistical typicality as a necessary condition for being part of human nature; it is therefore unsurprising that statistical typicality also features in Heyes's account: "human nature is the set of mechanisms that underlie the manifestation of species-typical cognitive and behavioral regularities, which humans tend to possess as a result of the evolution of the species" (Heyes 2018b, p. 215). Heyes rejects Machery's narrow conception of evolutionary processes and argues that some crucial components of human nature are culturally transmitted (and culturally evolved) cognitive gadgets. She claims that human nature "changes over historical, rather than geological time" (p. 216), but she retains the statistical-typicality requirement.

37 Cf. Baron-Cohen 2017; Pellicano and den Houting 2022.

38 For the full list of WEIRD psychological traits, see Henrich 2020, p. 57. In line with the Marxian account, the individualistic modes of life found in WEIRD societies are highly social modes of life.

39 Henrich (2020) refers to the role played by the Church's prohibition against cousin marriages. The Church benefited from the erosion of kin-based networks since this erosion facilitated the transfer of financial resources from Christian believers to the Church itself—primarily through wills.

40 It should be noted that Henrich (2020) presents some narratives in ways that betray a belief in the superiority of WEIRD dispositions. However, his psycho-historical hypotheses can be separated from this belief. Different evaluations of WEIRD dispositions are possible. Some might think that, to promote the common good, humans ought to become uniformly WEIRD, while others might contend that WEIRD attitudes are toxic and destructive, and ought to be eradicated. Some might claim that a blend of WEIRD and non-WEIRD dispositions is ideal, while others might suggest that both WEIRDness and its current alternatives need to be overcome. Some might assert that the WEIRD/non-WEIRD distinction is politically crucial, while others might argue that it is politically unhelpful. And so on.

41 Muthukrishna et al. 2021.

42 Henrich 2016, p. 66. Cooking is the most important of these skills, and it would not be possible without another set of culturally transmitted skills: those that enable humans to make and control fire; see Wrangham 2009.

43 Another example of how cultural processes, and thereby human praxis, can transform our bodies through the selection of favorable genetic variants involves the human thermoregulatory system. The evolution of this system was affected by the cultural transmission of knowledge about building water containers and finding water sources (Henrich 2016, pp. 71–8). Humans are “the sweatiest species”; but, unlike horses and camels, we cannot store large amounts of water inside our bodies; we use artifacts and culturally transmitted knowledge.

44 Wilson 1978, p. 242.

45 Cf. Boyd and Richerson 2008; Sterelny 2012; Henrich 2016; Laland 2017.

46 Boehm 1993; 1999; 2012; cf. also Boehm 1978; 1982.

47 Bonobos are an exception; see Wrangham 2019 and the discussion in Del Savio and Mameli 2020.

48 The debates on egalitarianism in small-scale human populations have changed significantly since the publication of Lewis H. Morgan’s book in 1877. On the fierce (but limited) egalitarianism of (some) hunter-gatherers, see Lee 1988; Woodburn 1982; Boehm 2012. Not all hunter-gatherers are egalitarian (cf. Graeber and Wengrow 2021), but this is compatible with the claim that many Late-Pleistocene hunter-gatherer bands, due to the interaction between human praxis and local circumstances, often had reverse-dominance arrangements, and with the view that those arrangements played a role in human evolution.

49 Boehm 1999.

50 Cf. Gintis et al. 2019. In a sense, then, Hobbes’s claims on mutual killability are not far from the truth.

51 de Waal 1996, pp. 91–2; cf. also de Waal 1982.

52 Boehm argues that ecological factors influenced the transgenerational stability of reverse-dominance hierarchies: in various circumstances, groups without reverse dominance were unlikely to survive; cf. Boehm 1999; Del Savio and Mameli 2020.

53 Boehm writes: “Group members’ punitive actions can not only influence group life but also shape gene pools in similar directions […]. Therefore, we must ask if some limited purposeful element is actually creeping into a biological evolutionary process that, in theory, is supposed to be operating ‘blindly’. […] [T]wo totally unambiguous and potent practical examples of purposeful selection would be animal breeders and modern genetic engineers. We must also include members of discredited eugenics movements, for the Nazis knew exactly what they were trying to accomplish.

All three consciously want to tamper with gene pools, and they all have some insight into what they are attempting. It's with good reason that we don't think of prehistoric hunter-gatherers as these kinds of active agents at all. Yet [...] unwittingly their social intentions did affect gene pools in ways that were predictable, highly significant, and at least were guided by rather sophisticated immediate purposes that had to do with improving their quality of life. Prehistorically, I believe that this provided a special 'focus' to the process of human social selection, a focus that derived from the very consistent practical purposes of the actors" (Boehm 2012, p. 16).

54 Wrangham 2019. Wrangham argues that a version of the *execution hypothesis* can be found in those passages where Darwin discusses the impact of punishment of criminals on human evolution (Darwin 1871, vol. 1, pp. 172–3). While Wrangham focuses on executions and genetic selection against aggression, Boehm (1999) suggests that milder forms of punishment also played a role, and that there was selection (possibly both cultural and genetic) not only against aggression but also in favor of (limited and conditional) cooperative and anti-authoritarian tendencies.

55 Wrangham argues that selection against reactive aggression in humans has produced paedomorphic traits: adult humans are in various respects (bones, muscles, and behavior) more like juvenile chimpanzees than like adult chimpanzees. According to Wrangham, these changes are an instance of a more general "domestication syndrome," which appears in mammals in response to selection against reactive aggression (Wrangham 2019). The thesis of a mammalian domestication syndrome comes from Belyaev 1979; 1984; cf. also Dugatkin and Trut 2017; Francis 2015. The debates about human domestication are explored in Del Savio and Mameli 2020.

56 Hrdy 2009; on the impact of human female strategies on human genetic evolution, see Hrdy 1990. There are links between Hrdy's hypotheses on cooperative breeding and the "grandmother hypothesis" (Hawkes 2020).

57 Knight 1991; cf. also Knight 2010; Knight and Power 2011.

58 On the term "human revolution": cf. Mellar and Stringer 1989. It is also worth noting that bonobos are less physically conflictual than chimpanzees and use sex as social glue and for conflict resolution. The distribution of this sexual social glue is to a large extent controlled by females, since in bonobos high-ranking adult females often rank higher than adult males. However, there are no sex strikes in bonobos. Chimpanzees and bonobos are the most closely related species to humans and are equally distant from our species in phylogenetic terms.

59 In some non-human primates, the highest-ranking (alpha) male and female often intervene in fights among group members to promote reconciliation (cf. von Rorh et al. 2012). Despite this, the level of physical conflict in these species is higher than in small-scale human groups. Arguably, when human groups were able to achieve sufficiently low levels of physical conflict—possibly, but not necessarily, through male-controlled or female-controlled reverse-dominance hierarchies—higher forms of productive cooperation emerged. When the tools of symbolic culture became available, new forms of peacekeeping became possible, alongside new conflicts.

60 For some of the relevant complexities, see, for instance, Sterelny 2021.

61 The literature on why the nature/culture divide needs to be abandoned keeps growing. However, these works rarely address in satisfactory ways the interconnections and interactions between human praxis and people's bodies and minds.

62 Cf. Lewens 2012a; see also the discussion in Lewens 2018.

63 Peter Godfrey-Smith writes: "If Martians came down and needed a *field guide* to the animals found on earth, there could be a useful field guide entry for our species—bipedal, relatively hairless, sociable, talkative. The Martians could recognize us by how we look and what we do. In that sense, there is surely nothing mythical about the idea of human nature" (Godfrey-Smith 2014, p. 139). This is interesting but problematic. In general, field guides only provide pictorial representations and short descriptions of traits that are easy to identify by sight (and, in some cases, sound). Moreover, most of the time, field guides only mention statistically typical traits, although, in some cases, they also refer to (perceptually salient) within-species differences (between gonadal males and females, for instance). In addition to the field guide, the Martians might want an atlas with detailed descriptions. However, even with this addition, the story is potentially misleading as it refers to an outside perspective, that of the Martians. Thinking about human nature in ways that take seriously the links between ideas about human nature and human praxis (human science included) requires acknowledging that what the Martians may find interesting about us (and about the ways we could be transformed) may be different from what is important from the point of view of our own conversations and decisions.

64 Some of the complexities emerge when we consider more specific questions: Should our way of thinking about human nature make room for bio-genealogical relations? If so, which ones? Should our way of thinking about human nature also make room for matters that cannot be captured by referring to "characters" or to bio-genealogical relations? If so, which ones? Should we also include aspects (if any) that cannot be the target of scientific research, broadly conceived?

65 Desmond and Moore argue that Darwin's abolitionist convictions not only motivated him to elaborate a unitarist view of human races, but also played a role in the development of the idea that all living beings are "netted together": "racial unity was [Darwin's] starting point for explaining the common descent of all life using a pedigree approach" (Desmond and Moore 2009, p. 126).

66 Darwin 1871, vol. 1, pp. 226–7.

67 Darwin writes: "As far as we are enabled to judge (although always liable to error on this head) not one of the external differences between the races of man are of any direct or special service to him" (Darwin 1871, vol. 1, pp. 248–9).

68 Darwin 1871, vol. 2, pp. 381–4. On sexual selection, see also M:32 in Darwin 1838b, N:26–28 in Darwin 1838–1839b.

69 On the distinction between "methodical" and "unconscious" artificial selection, see Darwin 1868; cf. Alter 2007; Del Savio and Mameli 2020. Through his discussion of artificial and sexual selection, Darwin shows that the adoption of evaluative standards can affect the evolutionary process. In relation to methodical selection in humans, Darwin mentions the case of the King of Prussia, who wanted tall grenadiers, and wanted his grenadiers to marry tall women, so as to have tall children who could then become grenadiers; the King, for a short period of time, introduced a new selection pressure (Darwin 1871, vol. 1, p. 112). In relation to humans and unconscious selection, see the brief comment in Darwin 1868, vol 1, p. 211.

70 Darwin 1871, vol. 1, pp. 248–9.

71 Darwin 1871, vol. 2, p. 405.

72 Darwin 1871, vol. 2, p. 404. Since I mentioned Rousseau's views on orangutans, I should also mention that Darwin, in one of his notebooks, makes this claim: "Compare, the Fuegian & the Ourang outang, & dare say the difference so great" (M:153 in Darwin 1838b). Darwin describes his interactions with the Fuegians in Darwin 1839; 1845. On Darwin's problematic views about the Fuegians, see Chapman 2010, Desmond and Moore 2009, Richards 2017.

73 Darwin writes: "In Tierra del Fuego, until some chief shall arise with power sufficient to secure any acquired advantages, such as the domesticated animals or other valuable presents, it seems scarcely possible that the political state of the country can be improved. At present, even a piece of cloth is torn into shreds and distributed; and no one individual becomes richer than another. On the other hand, it is difficult to understand how a chief can arise till there is property of some sort by which he might manifest and still increase his authority" (Darwin 1839, p. 242; 1845, pp. 229–30).

74 Darwin 1871, vol. 1, pp. 34–5; also p. 232. On human similarities in relation to mental faculties, cf. Darwin 1872. Four Fuegians (belonging to two different ethnic groups) were captured and taken to England during the *Beagle*'s first voyage (1826–30). One of them died of smallpox shortly after their arrival in England. The three who survived were taught English modes of life (including the English language) and were taken back to Tierra del Fuego during the *Beagle*'s second voyage (1831–6), where, to Darwin's surprise, they decided to stay; cf. Chapmen 2010.

75 Darwin writes: "As man advances in civilisation, and small tribes are united into larger communities, the simplest reason would tell each individual that he ought to extend his social instincts and sympathies to all the members of the same nation, though personally unknown to him. This point being once reached, there is only an artificial barrier to prevent his sympathies extending to the men of all nations and races. If, indeed, such men are separated from him by great differences in appearance or habits, experience unfortunately shews us how long it is before we look at them as our fellow-creatures. Sympathy beyond the confines of man, that is humanity to the lower animals, seems to be one of the latest moral acquisitions. It is apparently unfelt by savages, except towards their pets. How little the old Romans knew of it is shewn by their abhorrent gladiatorial exhibitions. The very idea of humanity, as far as I could observe, was new to most of the Gauchos of the Pampas. This virtue, one of the noblest with which man is endowed, seems to arise incidentally from our sympathies becoming more tender and more widely diffused, until they are extended to all sentient beings. As soon as this virtue is honoured and practised by some few men, it spreads through instruction and example to the young, and eventually through public opinion" (Darwin 1871, vol. 1, pp. 34–5; also p. 232).

76 Darwin 1871, vol. 1, p. 201; cf. also E:63–64 in Darwin 1838–1839a. Darwin argues that "Extinction [of human groups] follows chiefly from the competition of tribe with tribe, and race with race. […] The grade of civilisation seems a most important element in the success of nations which come in competition" (Darwin, vol. 1, pp. 238–9; cf. also p. 93, p. 98, p. 162; see also Darwin 1881b). Darwin hypothesizes that groups with higher levels of internal cooperation tend to outcompete groups with lower levels. Human evolution does not lead to the Hobbesian war of all against all, but to a war among tribes, with the more civilized vanquishing the less civilized. Some early commentators associated Darwin's view with the Hobbesian one (e.g., Gray 1860 and Huxley 1894); Kropotkin reacted to Huxley's claims on this matter by writing articles that eventually formed his book on mutual aid: Kropotkin 1902. For a contemporary take on the role that genetic and nongenetic group differences might have played in human evolution, see Bowles and Gintis 2011; Boyd and Richerson 2005.

77 Darwin 1871, vol. 2, p. 400.

78 Darwin 1871, vol. 1, p. 168, p. 174, p. 177.

79 Galton 1869; 1883, p. 24; 1909, p. 35; on eugenics, see Bashford and Levine 2010.

80 Darwin 1871, vol. 1, pp. 172–3.

81 Darwin 1871, vol. 1, pp. 177–8. The idea that progress is not an inevitable outcome of the evolutionary process is already present in Darwin's notebooks: N:47 in Darwin 1838–1839b. Both Darwin and Marx refer to "favourable" circumstances (or conditions) as required for human development, although they have different views about the occurrence and role of such circumstances.

82 Darwin 1871, vol. 1, pp. 168–9. It is also important to remember that Darwin experienced various health problems throughout his life. He expressed concerns about inbreeding affecting the health of his children, given that his wife Emma was also a first cousin of his.

83 Along with his views and attitudes on race and class, Darwin's ideological perspective on sex differences also needs to be mentioned. In *Descent*, Darwin argues that sexual selection operates in many species and much of his discussion focuses on birds. In numerous bird species, females "exert" their choice of partner, leading to males having nonadaptive traits selected by the females' aesthetic preferences. Darwin claims that, in our species, men are in control of partner choice, leaving women typically powerless (on this aspect of Darwin's account, see Richards 2017; Prum 2017; Rosenthal and Ryan 2022). Darwin argues that, due to differences in selection pressures, "man has ultimately become superior to woman" (Darwin 1871, vol. 2, p. 328). Alfred Russel Wallace, the co-discoverer of natural selection, disliked

Darwin's theory of sexual selection (Wallace 1864; 1870; see the discussion in Slotten 2004). In works published after Darwin's death, Wallace (who had become a socialist and a critic of Galtonian versions of eugenics) half-jokingly suggests that sexual selection did not affect human evolution in the past but might affect it in the future, when women become free to choose their husbands without being constrained by economic and social disadvantages: "When we allow ourselves to be guided by reason, justice, and public spirit in our dealings with our fellow-men, and determine to abolish poverty by recognising the equal rights of all the citizens of our common land to an equal share of the wealth which all combine to produce,—when we have thus solved the lesser problem of a rational social organisation adapted to secure the equal well-being of all, then we may safely leave the far greater and deeper problem of the improvement of the race to the cultivated minds and pure instincts of the Women of the Future" (Wallace 1890, p. 337; cf. also Wallace 1892; and the longer discussion in Wallace 1913).

84 Prum 2017; Zuk and Simmons 2018.

85 Darwin describes human "races" as "sub-species" (cf. Darwin 1871 vol. 1, p. 227 and p. 235; for a discussion, see Fuentes 2021). See James and Burgos 2020 for a summary of the debates on race eliminativism. Nowadays, from a praxis-centered perspective, we also have reasons to claim that erroneous beliefs about biological races have had a negative impact on various conversations and decisions about our modes of life.

86 The phrase "the monopoly of development" can be found in MECW, vol. 5, p. 431 [*German Ideology*]. For an in-depth discussion of Nietzsche's aristocratic elitism, see Losurdo 2019.

87 The claim that the idea of human moral equality plays a positive role in human praxis is not uncontroversial. It is rejected by various sorts of antihumanists, antispeciesists, posthumanists, Nietzscheans, and transhumanists.

88 It is useful to compare Darwin's claims about all living organisms being "netted together" with the Augustinian view. According to Augustine, for every non-human species, but not for humans, God "commanded that several should come into being at once." Therefore, while humans descend from a single original individual, the members of other species do not. God wanted all humans to descend from Adam because He wanted to "commend" to humans "the unity of society and the bond of concord" (Augustine 1998, 12.22): He wanted to "show mankind how highly He prized unity in a multitude" (12.23). Humans are "bound together not only by similarity of nature, but by the affection of kinship" (12.22). After the Last Judgment (when God becomes "all in all") the elect will be perfectly unified, in accordance with God's wishes (14.28; 1Cor. 15:28). Until then, according to Augustine, we should strive to create desirable forms of social unity, even though these efforts will be imperfect due to our fallen nature.

89 Darwin 1883, p. 3bv.

90 The phrase "Man in general" is used (polemically) in MECW, vol. 5, p. 360, and in MECW, vol. 6, p. 511.

91 Losurdo (2004, p. 123) argues that, for Hegel, "it is [...] the construction of the universal concept of man (or individual) that defines the progress of freedom, progress as such." Losurdo attributes the same view to Marx (Losurdo 2009, p. 41). Losurdo explains that within this framework the construction of a common humanity is not a mere intellectual matter: it requires "class struggles" and "struggles for recognition" (Losurdo 2016; Azzarà 2019). This construction can, in some circumstances, involve the elaboration of views about equal moral worth, but such views can be also used to promote exclusionary forms of human universalism (cf. Losurdo 2011; Losurdo 2016). While I am relying on (my elaboration of) Losurdo's formulations, alternative formulations are possible.

92 There are authors who characterize our common humanity as something that necessitates human praxis (including collective commitments) but argue that this characterization should be accompanied by the rejection of human-nature talk and of any reference to the biologicality of the human (cf. Phillips 2015; 2020; 2021; cf. also Smith 2020, ch. 8). In my view, an approach of this sort is theoretically as well as politically problematic. But it should be acknowledged that a pro-biology stance is not easy to articulate. One attempt worth mentioning is Theodosius Dobzhansky's. In 1946, Dunn and Dobzhansky wrote: "One of the most important facts about human beings is that they are not all alike. [...] Although they have equal rights, [humans] are assuredly not all alike" (Dunn and Dobzhansky 1946, pp. 1–2); and in 1973, Dobzhansky wrote: "It would seem that the easiest way to discredit the idea of equality is to show that people are innately, genetically, and therefore irremediably diverse and unlike. The snare is, of course, that human equality pertains to the rights and to the sacredness of life of every human being, not to bodily or even mental characteristics. [...] Defenders of equality become entangled in the same snare when they attempt to minimize or deny human genetic diversity. They overlook, or fail to understand, that diversity is an observable fact of nature, while equality is an ethical commandment" (Dobzhansky 1973, pp. 3–4; see also

Dobzhansky 1962, pp. 13–15). The problem with Dobzhansky's approach is that he did not have a satisfactory understanding of the relevant "ethical commandment" and of the role it can play in human praxis. The same can be said about other intellectuals who, more recently, have adopted a similar line (cf. Pinker 2002, ch. 8).

Conclusions

1 MECW, vol. 5, pp. 31–2, pp. 36–7, pp. 43–4 (translation modified; "mode of life" translates "*Lebensweise*"; "corporeal organisation" translates "*körperliche Organisation*"; "physical constitution" translates "*physische Beschaffenheit*"; cf. MEW bd. 3). In this text, Marx and Engels state the "premises" of the "materialist conception of history." They refer to the "*practical* materialist, i.e., the *communist,*" whose goal is that of "revolutionising the existing world" and of "practically coming to grips with and changing the things found in existence" (MECW, vol. 5, pp. 38–9). Debates about (what at the end of the nineteenth century came to be known as) "historical materialism" have often neglected the "corporeal organisation" and the "natural conditions" mentioned in *The German Ideology*; see the discussion in Fracchia 2022.

2 Gramsci 1992–2007, vol. 2, p. 11, translation modified, Q4§37 (cf. also Q11§64). This is Gramsci's way of distancing himself from Giovanni Gentile's actual-idealist account of the philosophy of praxis (Gentile 1916; 1922).

3 Gramsci 1992–2007, vol. 3, pp. 185–6, Q7§35 ("human differences" translates "*le differenze dell'uomo*"; "naturalistic timbre" translates "*carattere naturalistico*"; "human species" translates "*genere umano*").

4 MECW, vol. 5, p. 4, p. 7 [*Theses on Feuerbach*]; see Q16§12.

5 The sixth thesis and the divergent interpretations it has engendered are often at the center of the debates (mentioned earlier) on Marx's views on human nature.

6 Gramsci writes: "We can see that in putting the question 'what is man?' what we mean is: what can man become? That is, can man dominate his own destiny, can he 'make himself', can he create his own life? We maintain therefore that man is a process, and, more exactly, the process of his actions. […] It is necessary to reform the concept of man. I mean that one must conceive of man as a series of active relationships […]. The

humanity which is reflected in each individuality is composed of various elements: 1. the individual; 2. other men; 3. nature. But the latter two elements are not as simple as they might appear. […] Man does not enter into relations with nature just by being himself nature, but actively, by means of work and technique. Further: these relations are not mechanical. They are active and conscious. […] Some [of these relations] are necessary, others are voluntary. Further, to be conscious of them […] already modifies them. […] It is necessary to elaborate a doctrine in which these relations are seen as active and in movement, establishing quite clearly that the source of this activity is the consciousness of the individual man who knows, wishes, admires, creates, etc. and conceives of himself not as isolated but rich in the possibilities offered him by other men and by the society of things of which he cannot help having a certain knowledge" (Gramsci 1971, pp. 351–4; translation modified; Q10II§54).

7 Cf. Q4§45; Q11§62. In one passage, Gramsci concedes that, in addition to being the "ensemble of social conditions," "man is also the ensemble of his conditions of life"; even so, he insists, comparing humans of different historical epochs is "impossible, because one is dealing with different, if not heterogeneous, objects." He also writes: "Man is to be conceived as an historical bloc of purely individual and subjective elements and of mass and objective or material elements with which the individual is in an active relationship. To transform the external world, the general system of relations, is to potentiate oneself and to develop oneself. That ethical 'improvement' is purely individual is an illusion and an error: the synthesis of the elements constituting individuality is 'individual', but it cannot be realised and developed without an activity directed outward, modifying external relations both with nature and, in varying degrees, with other men, in the various social circles in which one lives, up to the greatest relationship of all, which embraces the whole human species. For this reason one can say that man is essentially 'political' since it is through the activity of transforming and consciously directing other men that man realises his 'humanity', his 'human nature'" (Gramsci 1971, pp. 359–60; Q10II§48; cf. also Q11§21, Q4§11). In another passage, after mentioning the distinction between "first nature" and "second nature," Gramsci suggests that what we call "first nature" may in fact be a second nature (Gramsci 1992–2007, vol. 2, p. 321, Q8§151). Passages like these need to be read alongside passages where Gramsci contends that there are "natural instincts" that are "primitive and animal," and that "education," "civilisation," and the "history of industrialism" can be seen as a "continuing struggle" against such instincts (cf. Gramsci 1971, p. 298, Q22§10; Q1§158).

8 Timpanaro 1982, p. 309; my translation.

9 Marx's version of the third thesis is in MECW, vol. 5, p. 4 (MEW bd. 3, p. 6); Engels's version is in MECW, vol. 5, p. 7 (MEW bd. 3, p. 354). Engels made various modifications to the text of the *Theses*, including other important changes to the text of the third thesis. Gramsci's translation of the *Theses* is in Q7. The phrase "*rovesciamento della praxis*" appears also in Q8§182, Q10II§33, Q10II§41, Q11§14. Gentile was the first to translate Engels's version of the *Theses* into Italian and translated "*umwälzende Praxis*" as "*praxis rovesciata*" (praxis overturned) and used also the expression "*prassi che si rovescia*" (praxis that overturns itself) (Gentile 1899, p. 59, p. 75, p. 80, p. 94, p. 98, p. 112). The phrase "*rovesciamento della praxis*" is used by Gentile in his discussion (pp. 111–4). It is also taken up by Mondolfo (1912) in his own discussion of historical materialism. Both Gentile and Mondolfo had an influence on Gramsci. Mustè (2021) explains how Gentile, Mondolfo, and Gramsci understood the overturning of praxis in different (but related) ways.

10 MECW, vol. 25, pp. 460–1 [*Dialectics of Nature*]. In a different section of the same work, Engels writes: "We find that there still exists here a colossal disproportion between the proposed aims and the results arrived at, that unforeseen effects predominate, and that the uncontrolled forces are far more powerful than those set into motion according to plan" (MECW, vol. 25, pp. 330–1).

11 Timpanaro 1975, pp. 41–2; see also p. 69; Timpanaro 2001, p. 211. On Engels and the historicity of nature, see for example MECW, vol. 40, p. 551; vol. 24, p. 467. On Marx, Engels, and Darwin, see Heyer 1982; Foster 2000; Mameli and Del Savio 2018. Engels read *On the Origin of Species* as soon as it was published. He remained a supporter of Darwinian ways of thinking for the rest of his life (as shown, for example, by the claims he made at Marx's funeral). He remained a supporter of Darwinian ways of thinking even when he saw the need to criticize what he called "bourgeois Darwinians." Engels had a more niche-constructionist understanding of Darwin's views than did Marx. As a result of this, Engels was in a better position to see how there could be room for revolutionary praxis within a broadly Darwinian framework and to understand how the transformative power of human praxis was conditioned by such a framework.

12 Timpanaro 2001, p. 211; cf. Timpanaro 1975, ch. 3. Addressing how Engels uses dialectics in his understanding of nature is beyond the scope of this discussion; cf. Levins and Lewontin 1985; Sheehan 1993; Thomas 2021; Foster 2020. Timpanaro points out that a radically non-dialectical conception of nature is present in Giacomo Leopardi's work (Timpanaro

1975; 1982; 1995; 2001; see also Pestelli 2013; Williams 1980). What Timpanaro calls "my initial and fragmentary Marxism-Leopardism" (Timpanaro 1975, p. 10)—a fusion of Leopardian and Engelsian insights—deserves more attention than it has received.

13 Engels points out that at some point "matter [...] will exterminate on the earth its highest creation, the thinking mind" (MECW, vol. 25, p. 335; see the whole passage pp. 331–5 [*Dialectics of Nature*]). He explains how to understand the kind of "mastery" to which we can aspire: "Freedom does not consist in any dreamt-of independence from natural laws, but in the knowledge of these laws, and in the possibility this gives of systematically making them work towards definite ends. This holds good in relation both to the laws of external nature and to those which govern the bodily and mental existence of men themselves—two classes of laws which we can separate from each other at most only in thought but not in reality" (MECW, vol. 25, p. 104 [*Anti-Dühring*]).

14 Timpanaro 1975, p. 11.

15 Timpanaro 1975, p. 103, p. 171, p. 172. Timpanaro attacks scientistic anti-materialism, but also argues that the bourgeois aspects of "bourgeois science" need to be properly addressed (see Timpanaro 1976, pp. 173–5, and more generally the discussion in ch. 11 of that book). The expression "bourgeois science" is used by Engels (e.g., in MECW, vol. 25, p. 212).

16 Gramsci 1992–2007, vol. 2, p. 242; Q4§71, Q11§39; see also Q8§215; Q11§17.

17 Cf. Q11§27; Q4§7, Q11§38; see the discussion in Timpanaro 1975, p. 242; see also what Marx and Engels say on "self-sufficient philosophy" in MECW, vol. 5, p. 37 [*German Ideology*]. It should be noted that the manuscript of *The German Ideology*, written in 1846, was published in 1932. Gramsci could not read the full work but was able to read some sections or summaries (Antonini 2018). Gramsci argues that Marxism, when reconstructed in the terms of a philosophy of praxis, is a genuine philosophical outlook rather than just an economic and sociological theory. He wants the philosophy of praxis to be "independent and original philosophy" (Q4§3); see also Q4§25, Q11§30, and (in Q7) Gramsci's translation of Marx's preface to "A contribution to the critique of political economy," containing also Marx's comment on the role of natural science; cf. MECW, vol. 29, p. 263.

18 "Some aspects of the Southern Question," in Gramsci 1978; Gramsci 1991. Gramsci was arrested on November 8, 1926.

19 Gramsci 1978, p. 444; for a slightly different translation, see Gramsci 1994, pp. 316–17.

20 Gramsci 1992–2007, vol. 1, pp. 143–4; Q1§44; cf. Q19§24.

21 Gramsci takes issue with a book where "Sardinians are called *monkeys*" (Gramsci 1992–2007, vol. 1, p. 162, Q1§50; see also the claims on the treatment of the Sardinian population in Q23§54).

22 See "I dolori della Sardegna" (1919), now in Gramsci 2008 (in particular, the discussion of Sardinia and Eritrea on p. 75). See also "Gli scopritori" (1916), and other writings collected in Gramsci 2008. For a discussion, see Fiori 1990, especially ch. 9; Lussana 2006; Fresu 2022, ch. 15.

23 Another issue that needs to be explored is the way Gramsci's theorizing relates to his health problems, disability, and physical deformity. Gramsci had spinal tuberculosis (Pott's disease), which first appeared during his childhood and affected him for the rest of his life. Illness and disability, as Timpanaro explains, are a part of nature with which we need to come to grips when we form our reflective conception of the world. Giacomo Leopardi, whose insights Timpanaro seeks to incorporate into his own materialism, also suffered from spinal tuberculosis. On Gramsci's biography and illness (and on Leopardi having the same condition) see for example D'Orsi 2018. See Forgacs 2016 on Gramsci's deformity and the ways in which he has been politically and theoretically "undisabled."

24 Gramsci contends that, despite the fact that science is an "ideology" and a "superstructure," "one group can appropriate the science of another group without accepting its ideology" (Gramsci 1992–2007, vol. 2, pp. 149–50; Q4§7; Q11§38; see also Q4§47, Q11§34). This statement can be compared with these ones by Labriola and Timpanaro, respectively: "This science, which the bourgeois epoch has, through its inherent conditions, stimulated and made to grow like a giant, is the only heritage of past centuries which communism accepts and adopts without reserve" (Labriola 1903, p. 215; Labriola 1965, p. 132); "A polemic against science (as distinct from false science or capitalist use of science) is a counsel of despair. A scientific communism [...] signifies a scientific relationship to bourgeois science. The latter [...] is not totally ideological but has a genuine scientific content which reveals an objective reality, that as such is in a certain sense always 'neutral'—even if the practical need which motivates any given programme of research is anything but neutral, as is not only the use made of scientific research (by ourselves or the bourgeoisie), but also the organisation of scientific research itself, and the participation or exclusion of non-specialists in it" (Timpanaro 1976, pp. 173–5). The three statements are similar and different in important ways. Another interesting assertion made by Gramsci is that "experimental science [...] is the cultural element that has contributed the most to unifying humanity" (Gramsci 1992–2007, vol. 3, p. 337, Q8§177; Q11§17). Gramsci claims that we should study the natural sciences in order to demystify them through a historical understanding of their role in human life and politics (cf. Q4§77; Q12§2; see also Q6§166; Q6§180; Q7§38). In Q11§15, he asserts that "one needs to critically destroy" common ways of thinking about science. On Gramsci and the experimental sciences, see Sclocco 2021; on Gramsci's ways of thinking about ideology (and science), see Liguori 2004; Filippini 2012.

25 MECW, vol. 11, p. 103.

26 MECW, vol. 11, p. 104.

27 Cf. Wilson 1978, p. 80. Limitationist ideas can also be found, for example, in Singer 1999 and Pinker 2002; 2011. Wilson (1978) argues that human nature (which in his account includes some genetically caused phenotypic differences) makes certain projects often considered emancipatory unlikely to succeed. In this context, he discusses projects aimed at reducing gender differences. Interestingly, Wilson also argues that (what he conceives of as) our genetically fixed human nature makes human slavery an unstable institution.

28 For the potentialist view, see Gould 1978; Lewontin et al. 1984. For the contrast between limitationist and potentialist approaches, see the discussion in Berry 1986, ch. 7 and ch. 8.

29 Similarly, artificial wombs for ectogestation (or ectogenesis) might soon create new dynamics and patterns in relation to old and socially mediated differences between humans who can internally gestate a fetus and humans who cannot. These new dynamics and patterns will impact the web of social conflicts; cf. Hester 2018; Firestone 1970; Haldane 1923; Cavaliere 2019.

30 Darwin 1794–1796, vol. 1, p. 183. The first volume of *Zoonomia* was published fifteen years before Charles Darwin's birth in 1809 and eighty-seven years before the publication of Darwin's book on earthworms. Erasmus was also Francis Galton's grandfather: Erasmus had Charles's father with his first wife and Francis's mother with his second wife.

31 The interview (by Luca Lamberti) took place in 1971. It can be found in Levi 2001, in the chapter "*Science Fiction: Il vizio di forma.*"

References

Adamson P, Rapp C (eds.). 2021. *State and nature*. De Gruyter.

Agamben G. 2003. *The open*. Stanford University Press.

Agamben G. 2010. *Nudities*. Stanford University Press.

Agamben G. 2017. *The omnibus homo sacer*. Stanford University Press.

Agamben G. 2020. *The kingdom and the garden*. Seagull.

Akino T, Nakamura K, Wakamura S. 2004. Diet-induced chemical phytomimesis by twig-like caterpillars of Biston robustum Butler (Lepidoptera: Geometridae). *Evolutionary, mechanistic and environmental approaches to chemically-mediated interactions* 14, pp. 165–74.

Alter S. 2007. Separated at birth: the interlinked origins of Darwin's unconscious selection concept and the application of sexual selection to race. *Journal of the History of Biology* 40, pp. 231–58.

Althusser L. 2005. *For Marx*. Verso.

Althusser L, Balibar E, Establet R, Macherey P, Ranciere J. 2015. *Reading Capital*. Verso.

Anderson K. 2010. *Marx at the margins*. University of Chicago Press.

Antonini F. 2018. Gramsci, il materialism storico e l'antologia russa del 1924. *Studi storici* 59:2, pp. 403–36.

Aravamudan S. 2009. Hobbes and America. D Carey, L Festa (eds.), *Postcolonial Enlightenment* (pp. 37–69). Oxford University Press.

Arendt H. 1958. *The human condition*. University of Chicago Press.

Aristotle. 1926. *Nicomachean ethics*. Harvard University Press.

Aristotle. 1932. *Politics*. Harvard University Press.

Aristotle. 1935. *Eudemian ethics*. Harvard University Press.

Aristotle. 1965–1991. *History of animals*. Harvard University Press.

Aristotle. 2011. *Problems*. Harvard University Press.

Atran S, Estin P, Coley J, Medin D. 1997. Generic species and basic levels: essence and appearance in folk biology. *Journal of Ethnobiology* 17, pp. 17–43.

Augustine. 1957. *Against Julian*. Catholic University of America Press.

Augustine. 1998. *The city of God*. Cambridge University Press.
Azzarà S. 2019. *La comune umanità*. Scuola di Pitagora.
Badiou P. 2019. *I know there are so many of you*. Polity.
Baker F. 1998. Rousseau and the colonies. *Eighteenth-Century Life* 22:1, pp. 172–89.
Barnes E. 2015. *The minority body*. Oxford University Press.
Baron-Cohen S. 2017. Neurodiversity – a revolutionary concept for autism and psychiatry. *Journal of Child Psychology and Psychiatry* 58:6, pp. 744–7.
Bashford A, Levine P. 2010. *Oxford handbook of the history of eugenics*. Oxford University Press.
Bateson P. 1991. Are there principles of behavioural development? P Bateson (ed.), *The development and integration of behaviour*. Cambridge University Press.
Beauvoir S. (de). 2009. *The second sex*. Cape.
Belyaev DK. 1979. Destabilizing selection as a factor in domestication. *Journal of Heredity* 70:5, pp. 301–8.
Belyaev DK. 1984. Genetics, society and personality. VL Chopra, BC Joshi, RP Sharma, HC Bausal (eds.), *Genetics: new frontiers* (pp. 383–5). Oxford University Press and IBH.
Benjamin W. 1969. *Illuminations*. Schocken.
Bergström A. et al. 2020. Insights into human genetic variation and population history from 929 diverse genomes. *Science* 367:6484, aay5012.
Berkow J, Cosmides L, Tooby J (eds.). 1992. *The adapted mind*. Oxford University Press.
Berry CJ. 1986. *Human nature*. Macmillan.
Boehm C. 1978. Rational preselection from Hamadryas to Homo Sapiens: the place of decisions in adaptive process. *American Anthropologist* 80, pp. 265–96.
Boehm C. 1982. The evolutionary development of morality as an effect of dominance behavior and conflict interference. *Journal of Social and Biological Structures* 5, pp. 413–22.
Boehm C. 1993. Egalitarian behavior and reverse dominance hierarchy. *Current Anthropology* 34, pp. 227–54.
Boehm C. 1999. *Hierarchy in the forest*. Harvard University Press.
Boehm C. 2012. *Moral origins*. Basic Books.
Bowles S, Gintis H. 2011. *A cooperative species*. Princeton University Press.
Boyd R. 1999. Homeostasis, species, and higher taxa. R Wilson (ed.), *Species* (pp. 141–86). MIT Press.
Boyd R, Richerson J. 2005. *The origin and evolution of cultures*. Oxford University Press.
Boyd R, Richerson J. 2008. *Not by genes alone*. University of Chicago Press.

Braidotti R, Hlavajova M (eds.). 2018. *Posthuman glossary*. Bloomsbury.
Bramhall J. 1844. *The works of the most Reverend Father in God, John Bramhall*, vol. IV. Parker.
Buchanan A. 2011. *Beyond humanity?* Oxford University Press.
Buchanan A, Brock D, Daniels N, Wikler D. 2001. *From chance to choice*. Oxford University Press.
Buller DJ. 2005. *Adapting minds*. MIT Press.
Burgess A, Cappelen H, Plunkett D (eds.) 2020. *Conceptual engineering and conceptual ethics*. Oxford University Press.
Buss LW. 1988. *The evolution of individuality*. Princeton University Press.
Butler J. 1990. *Gender trouble*. Routledge.
Butler J. 1993. *Bodies that matter*. Routledge.
Cagnoli Fiecconi E. 2021. Elements of biology in Aristotle's political science. *Cambridge companion to Aristotle's biology* (pp. 211–27). Cambridge University Press.
Candioti M. 2022. Praxis. B Skeggs, S Farris, A Toscano, S Bromberg (eds.), *The SAGE Handbook of Marxism* (pp. 543–58). SAGE.
Caplan AR (ed.). 1978. *The sociobiology debate*. Harper.
Cavaliere G. 2019. Gestation, equality and freedom: ectogenesis as a political perspective. *Journal of medical ethics* 46:2, pp. 76–82.
Chalmers DJ. 2020. What is conceptual engineering and what should it be? *Inquiry*.
Chapman A. 2010. *European encounters with the Yamana people of Cape Horn before and after Darwin*. Cambridge University Press.
Chappell T. 2009. "Naturalism" in Aristotle's political philosophy. RK Balot (ed.), *A companion to Greek and Roman political thought* (pp. 382–98). Wiley-Blackwell.
Chomsky N. 1959. Review of *Verbal behavior*. *Language* 35, pp. 26–58.
Chomsky N, Foucault M. 1974. Human nature: justice versus power. F Elder (ed.), *Reflexive waters* (pp. 133–97). Souvenir Press.
Coccia E. 2020. *Métamorphoses*. Rivages.
Cohen G, Kymlicka W. 1988. Human nature and social change in the Marxist conception of history. *Journal of Philosophy* 85:4, pp. 171–91.
Cova L. 2014. *Peccato originale*. Mulino.
Crespi BJ, Yanega D. 1995. The definition of eusociality. *Behavioral Ecology* 6:1, pp. 109–15.
Cribb R, Gilbert H, Tiffin H. 2014. *Wild man from Borneo*. University of Hawai'i Press.
Darwin C. 1837–1838. Notebook B: [Transmutation of species]. Darwin Online, http://darwin-online.org.uk (J van Wyhe, ed.), CUL–DAR121.

Darwin C. 1838a. On the formation of mould. *Proceedings of the Geological Society of London* 2, pp. 574–6.

Darwin C. 1838b. Notebook M: [Metaphysics on morals and speculations on expression]. Darwin Online, http://darwin-online.org.uk (P Barrett, J van Wyhe, eds.), CUL–DAR125.

Darwin C. 1838–1839a. Notebook E: [Transmutation of species]. Darwin Online, http://darwin-online.org.uk (J van Wyhe, ed.), CUL–DAR124.

Darwin C. 1838–1839b. Notebook N: [Metaphysics and expression]. Darwin Online, http://darwin-online.org.uk (P Barrett, J van Wyhe, eds.), CUL–DAR126.

Darwin C. 1839. *Narrative of the surveying voyages of His Majesty's Ships Adventure and Beagle between the years 1826 and 1836 – Volume III: Journal and remarks, 1832-1836*. Colburn.

Darwin C. 1843. Letter to GR Waterhouse, July 26, 1843. *Darwin Correspondence Project*, DCP-LETT-684.

Darwin C. 1845. *Journal of researches into the natural history and geology of the countries visited during the voyage of H.M.S. Beagle round the world; second edition, corrected, with additions*. Murray.

Darwin C. 1851a. *A monograph of the sub-class Cirripedia, with figures of all the species. The Lepadidæ; or, pedunculated cirripedes*. Ray Society.

Darwin C. 1851b. *A monograph on the fossil Lepadidæ, or pedunculated cirripedes of Great Britain*. Palæontographical Society.

Darwin C. 1854a. *A monograph on the sub-class Cirripedia, with figures of all the species. The Balanidæ, (or sessile cirripedes); the Verrucidæ, etc. etc. etc.* Ray Society.

Darwin C. 1854b. *A monograph on the fossil Balanidæ and Verrucidæ of Great Britain*. Palæontographical Society.

Darwin C. 1859. *On the origin of species by means of selection, or the preservation of favoured races in the struggle for life*. Murray.

Darwin C. 1868. *The variation of animals and plants under domestication*. Murray.

Darwin C. 1869. The formation of mould by worms. *Gardeners' Chronicle and Agricultural Gazette* 20, p. 530.

Darwin C. 1871. *The descent of man and selection in relation to sex*. Murray.

Darwin C. 1872. *The expression of the emotions in man and animals*. Murray.

Darwin C. 1881a. *The formation of vegetable mould, through the action of worms, with observation of their habits*. Murray.

Darwin C. 1881b. Letter to William Graham, July 3, 1881. *Darwin Correspondence Project*, DCP-LETT-13230.

Darwin E. 1794–1796. *Zoonomia, or the laws of organic life*. Johnson.

Darwin F. 1887. *The life and letters of Charles Darwin, including an autobiographical chapter*. Murray.

Darwin W. 1883. Recollections of Charles Darwin. Darwin Online, http://darwin-online.org.uk (J van Wyhe, ed.), CUL-DAR112.B3b–B3f.

de Waal F. 1982. *Chimpanzee politics*. Harper & Row.

de Waal F. 1996. *Good natured*. Harvard University Press.

de Waal F. 2022. *Different*. Granta.

Del Savio L, Mameli M. 2020. Human domestication and the roles of human agency in human evolution. *History and Philosophy of the Life Sciences* 42:2, article 21.

Dennett D. 1995. *Darwin's dangerous idea*. Simon & Schuster.

Depew D. 1995. Humans and other political animals in Aristotle's History of Animals. *Phronesis* 40, pp. 156–81.

Depew D. 2009. The ethics of Aristotle's *Politics*. RK Balot (ed.), *A companion to Greek and Roman political thought* (pp. 399–417). Wiley-Blackwell.

Depew D. 2019. Political animals and the genealogy of the *polis*: Aristotle's *Politics and* Plato's *Statesman*. G Keil, N Kreft (eds.), *Aristotle's anthropology* (pp. 238–57). Cambridge University Press.

Derrida J. 2009. *The beast and the sovereign: volume I*. University of Chicago Press.

Desmond A, Moore J. 1992. *Darwin*. Penguin.

Desmond A, Moore J. 2009. *Darwin's sacred cause*. Houghton Mifflin Harcourt.

Devitt M. 2008. Resurrecting biological essentialism. *Philosophy of Science* 75, pp. 344–82.

Devitt M. 2010. Species have (partly) intrinsic essences. *Philosophy of Science* 77, pp. 648–61.

Devitt M. 2021. Defending intrinsic biological essentialism. *Philosophy of Science* 88, pp. 67–82.

D'Orsi A. 2018. *Antonio Gramsci*. Feltrinelli.

Dobzhansky T. 1962. *Mankind evolving*. Yale University Press.

Dobzhansky T. 1973. *Genetic diversity and human equality*. Basic Books.

Dudley JS, Hannaford P, Dowland SN, Lindsay LA, Thompson MB, Murphy CR, Van Dyke CJ, Whittington CM. 2021. Structural changes to the brood pouch of male pregnant seahorses (Hippocampus abdominalis) facilitate exchange between father and embryos. *Placenta* 114, pp. 115–23.

Dugatkin LA, Trut LN. 2017. *How to tame a fox*. University of Chicago Press.

Dunn LC, Dobzhansky T. 1946. *Heredity, race, and society*. Penguin.

Dupré J. 2015. Pluralism and process in understanding human nature. *Rivista di filosofia neoscolastica* 107, pp. 1–2, 15–24.

Ellis EC. 2018. *Anthropocene*. Oxford University Press.

Ereshefsky M. 2010. What's wrong with the new biological essentialism. *Philosophy of Science* 77:5, pp. 674–85.
Ereshefsky M, Matthen M. 2005. Taxonomy, polymorphism, and history: an introduction to population structure theory. *Philosophy of Science* 72:1, pp. 1–21.
Fanon F. 1967. *Black skin, white mask*. Grove Press.
Fausto-Sterling A. 2000. *Sexing the body*. Basic Books.
Fausto-Sterlling A. 2012. *Sex/gender*. Routledge.
Feenberg A. 2014. *The philosophy of praxis*. Verso.
Ferrando T. 2013. Posthumanism, transhumanism, antihumanism, metahumanism, and new materialisms. *Existenz* 8:2, pp. 26–32.
Filippini M. 2012. Tra scienze e senso comune: dell'ideologia in Gramsci. *Scienza & Politica* XXV:47, pp. 89–106.
Finelli R. 1999. Gramsci filosofo della prassi. G Baratta, G Liguori (eds.), *Gramsci da un secolo all'altro* (pp. 188–98). Editori Riuniti.
Fiori G. 1990. *Antonio Gramsci: Life of a revolutionary*. Verso.
Firestone S. 1970. *The dialectic of sex*. Morrow.
FitzRoy R. 1839. *Narrative of the surveying voyages of His Majesty's Ships Adventure and Beagle between the years 1826 and 1836 – Volume II: Proceedings of the second expedition, 1831-1836*. Colburn.
Fluss H, Frim L. 2022. *Prometheus and Gaia*. Anthem.
Foster JB. 2000. *Marx's ecology*. Monthly Review.
Foster JB. 2020. *The return of nature*. Monthly Review.
Forgacs D. 2016. Gramsci undisabled. *Modern Italy* 21:4, pp. 345–60.
Forster JB. 2022. *Capitalism in the Anthropocene*. Monthly Review.
Foster KR, Ratnieks FLW. 2000. Conflict resolution in insect societies. *Nature* 407, pp. 692–3.
Fox J. 2016. *Marx, the body and human nature*. Palgrave Macmillan.
Fracchia J. 2022. *Bodies and artefacts*. Brill.
Francis RC. 2015. *Domesticated*. Norton.
Fresu G. 2022. *Antonio Gramsci*. Palgrave.
Frosini F. 2004. Filosofia della praxis. F Frosini, G Liguori (eds.), *Le parole di Gramsci* (pp. 93–111). Carocci.
Fuentes A. 2021. "On the races of man": race, racism, science and hope. J DeSilva (ed.), *A most interesting problem: what Darwin's Descent of Man got right and wrong about human evolution* (pp. 183–203). Princeton University Press.
Fukuyama F. 2002. *Our posthuman future*. Straus & Giroux.
Galton F. 1869. *Hereditary genius*. Macmillan.
Galton F. 1883. *Inquiries into human faculty and development*. Macmillan.
Galton F. 1909. *Essays on eugenics*. Eugenics Education Society.

Garland-Thomson R. 2012. The case for conserving disability. *Journal of bioethical enquiry* 9, pp. 339–55.
Garland-Thomson R. 2015. Human biodiversity conservation: a consensual ethical principle. *American Journal of Bioethics* 15:6, pp. 13–15.
Gedik AC. 2022. Back to Engels. *Marxism and Sciences* 1:1, pp. xii–xxxix.
Gelman S. 2004. Psychological essentialism in children. *Trends in Cognitive Science* 8:9, pp. 404–9.
Gentile G. 1899. *La filosofia di Marx*. Spoerri.
Gentile G. 1916. *Teoria generale dello spirito come atto puro*. Mariotti.
Gentile G. 1922. *The theory of mind as pure act*. Macmillan.
Geras N. 1983. *Marx and human nature*. Verso.
Ghetti N. 2014. *Gramsci nel cieco carcere degli eretici*. Asino d'oro.
Ghiselin M. 1997. *Metaphysics and the origin of species*. SUNY Press.
Gintis H, van Schaik C, Boehm C. 2019. Zoon politikon: The evolutionary origins of human socio-political systems. *Behavioral Processes* 161, pp. 17–30.
Godfrey-Smith P. 2004. *Complexity and the function of mind in nature*. Cambridge University Press.
Godfrey-Smith P. 2009. *Darwinian populations and natural selection*. Oxford University Press.
Godfrey-Smith P. 2014. *Philosophy of biology*. Princeton University Press.
Godfrey-Smith P, Sterelny K. 2016. Biological information. *Stanford Encyclopedia of Philosophy*, https://plato.stanford.edu.
Godman M, Mallozzi A, Papineau D. 2020. Essential properties are super-explanatory: taming metaphysical modality. *Journal of the American Philosophical Association* 6:3, pp. 316–34.
Godman M, Papineau D. 2020. Species have historical not intrinsic essences. A Bianchi (ed.), *Language and reality from a naturalistic perspective* (pp. 355–67). Springer.
Godwin J. 2010. Neuroendocrinology of sexual plasticity in teleost fishes. *Frontiers in Neuroendocrinology* 31:2, pp. 203–16.
Gould SJ. 1978. Biological potential vs biological determinism. AR Caplan (ed.), *The sociobiology debate*. Harper.
Graeber D, Wengrow D. 2021. *The dawn of everything*. Farrar, Straus & Giroux.
Gramsci A. 1960. *Sotto la mole*. Einaudi.
Gramsci A. 1971. *Selections from the prison notebooks* (Q Hoare, G Nowell-Smith, eds.). International Publishers.
Gramsci A. 1973. *Letters from prison* (L Lawner, ed.). Harper & Row.
Gramsci A. 1975a. *Quaderni del carcere* (V Gerratana, ed.). Einaudi.
Gramsci A. 1975b. *Scritti giovanili (1914–1918)*. Einaudi.

Gramsci A. 1977. *Selections from political writings (1910–1920)* (Q Hoare, ed.). Lawrence & Wishart.

Gramsci A. 1978. *Selections from political writings (1921–1926)* (Q Hoare, ed.). Lawrence & Wishart.

Gramsci A. 1991. *La questione meridionale*. Editori Riuniti.

Gramsci A. 1992–2007. *Prison notebooks* (JA Buttigieg, ed.). Columbia University Press.

Gramsci A. 1994. *Pre-prison writings* (R Bellamy, ed.). Cambridge University Press.

Gramsci A. 1995. *Further selections from the prison notebooks* (D Boothman, ed.). Lawrence & Wishart.

Gramsci A. 1996. *Lettere dal carcere* (A Santucci, ed.). Sellerio.

Gramsci A. 2008. *Scritti sulla Sardegna* (G Melis, ed.). Ilisso.

Gray A. 1860. Review of Darwin's theory on the origin of species by means of natural selection. *American Journal of Science and Arts* 2:29, pp. 153–84.

Gray RD. 1992. Death of the gene: Developmental systems strike back. PE Griffiths (ed.), *Trees of life* (pp. 165–210). Kluwer.

Gray RD. 2001. Selfish genes or developmental systems? R Singh, K Krimbas, D Paul, J Beatty (eds.), *Thinking about evolution* (pp. 184–207). Cambridge University Press.

Griffiths PE. 1999. Squaring the circle: natural kinds with historical essences. R Wilson (ed.), *Species* (pp. 209–28). MIT Press.

Griffiths PE. 2011. Our plastic nature. SB Gissis, E Jablonka (eds.), *Transformations of Lamarckism* (pp. 319–30). MIT Press.

Griffiths PE, Gray RD. 1994. Developmental systems and evolutionary explanation. *Journal of Philosophy* 91:6, pp. 277–304.

Griffiths PE, Gray RD. 2001. Darwinism and developmental systems. S Oyama, PE Griffiths, RD Gray (eds.), *Cycles of Contingency* (pp. 195–218). MIT Press.

Habermas J. 2003. *The future of human nature*. Polity.

Haldane JBS. 1923. *Daedalus*. Kagan Paul, Trench, Trauber & Co.

Hamilton J. 2009. Hobbes the royalist, Hobbes the republican. *History of Political Thought* 30:3, pp. 411–54.

Hanke L. 1951. *Bartolomé de Las Casas*. Springer.

Hanke L. 1959. *Aristotle and the American Indians*. Indiana University Press.

Haraway D. 1990. *Simians, cyborgs, and women*. Routledge.

Haraway D. 2016. *Staying with the trouble*. Duke University Press.

Harden K. 2021. *The genetic lottery*. Princeton University Press.

Harris J. 2010. *Enhancing evolution*. Princeton University Press.

Haslam N. 2017. The origins of lay theories: the case of essentialist beliefs. C Zedelius, C Müller, J Schooler (eds.), *The science of lay theories* (pp. 3–16). Springer.

Haslam N, Loughnan S. 2014. Dehumanization and infrahumanization. *Annual Reviews of Psychology* 65, pp. 399–423.
Hawkes K. 2020. The centrality of ancestral grandmothering in human evolution. *Integrative and Comparative Biology* 60:30, pp. 765–81.
Heidegger M. 1977. Letter on humanism. DF Krell (ed.), *Basic writings*. Harper and Row.
Heidegger M. 2014. *Introduction to metaphysics*. Yale University Press.
Helanterä H, Ratnieks FLW. 2010. Worker-worker conflict and worker policing. MD Breed, J Moore (eds.), *Encyclopedia of Animal Behavior* (pp. 621–8). Academic Press.
Henrich J. 2016. *The secret of our success*. Princeton University Press.
Henrich J. 2020. *The weirdest people in the world*. Allen Lane.
Hester H. 2018. *Xenofeminism*. Polity.
Heyer P. 1982. *Nature, human nature, and society*. Greenwood.
Heyes C. 2018a. Human nature, natural pedagogy, and evolutionary causal essentialism. E Hannon, T Lewens (eds.), *Why we disagree about human nature* (pp. 76–91). Oxford University Press.
Heyes C. 2018b. *Cognitive gadgets*. Harvard University Press.
Hirschman NJ. 2016. Hobbes on the family. HP Martinich, K Hoekstra (eds.), *Oxford Handbook to Hobbes* (pp. 242–63). Oxford University Press.
Hobbes T. 1642. *Elementorum philosophiae section tertia de cive*. Paris.
Hobbes T. 1839–1845. *The English works of Thomas Hobbes* (W Molesworth, ed.). Bohm.
Hobbes T. 1983. *De Cive: the Latin version* (H Warrender, ed.). Clarendon.
Hobbes T. 1997. *On the citizen* (R Tuck, ed.). Cambridge University Press.
Hobbes T. 1998. *Man and citizen* (B Gert, ed.). Hackett.
Hobbes T. 2012. *Leviathan* (N Malcom, ed.). Clarendon.
Hobbes T. 2017. *Three-text edition of T Hobbes's political theory* (D Baumgold, ed.). Cambridge University Press.
Hölldobler B, Wilson EO. 2009. *The superorganism*. Norton.
Hrdy S. 1990. *The woman that never evolved*. Harvard University Press.
Hrdy S. 2009. *Mothers and others*. Harvard University Press.
Hull D. 1978. A matter of individuality. *Philosophy of Science* 45, pp. 335–60.
Hull D. 1986. On human nature. *PSA: Proceedings of the Biennial Meeting of the Philosophy of Science Association* 2, pp. 3–13.
Hull D. 1994. Contemporary systematic philosophies. E Sober (ed.), *Conceptual issues in evolutionary biology*, 2nd edition (pp. 295–330). MIT Press.
Huxley T. 1894. *Evolution and ethics, and other essays*. Macmillan.
Isaac MG, Koch S. 2022. Foundational issues in conceptual engineering: introduction and overview. *Inquiry*.

Jablonski N. 2018. Skin color. W Trevathan (ed.). *The international encyclopedia of biological anthropology*. Wiley.

James M, Burgos A. 2020. Race. *Stanford Encyclopedia of Philosophy*, https:// plato.stanford.edu.

Kaessmann H, Wiebe V, Weiss G, Pääbo S. 2021. Great ape DNA sequences reveal a reduced diversity and an expansion in humans. *Nature Genetics* 22, pp. 155–6.

Karbowki J. 2019. Political animals and human nature in Aristotle's *Politics*. G Keil, N Kreft (eds.), *Aristotle's anthropology* (pp. 221–37). Cambridge University Press.

Kelly C. 2006. Rousseau's "peut-etre": reflections on the status of the state of nature. *Modern Intellectual History* 3:1, pp. 75–83.

Kitcher P. 2001. Battling the undead: How (and how not) to resist genetic determinism. R Singh, K Krimbas, D Paul, J Beatty (eds.), *Thinking about evolution* (pp. 396–414). Cambridge University Press.

Knight C. 1991. *Blood relations*. Yale University Press.

Knight C. 2010. The origins of symbolic culture. U Frey, C Stormer, KP Willfuhr (eds.), *Homo novus* (pp. 193–211). Springer.

Knight C, Power C. 2011. Social conditions for the evolutionary emergence of language. M Tallerman, K Gibson (eds.), *Handbook of language evolution* (pp. 346–9). Oxford University Press.

Knoll M. 2017. Aristotle's arguments for his political anthropology and the natural existence of the *polis*. R Güremen, A Jaulin (eds.), *Aristote: l'animal politique*. Èditions de la Sorbonne.

Kronfeldner M. 2016. The politics of human nature. M Timbayrenc, E Ayala (eds.), *On human nature*. Academic Press.

Kronfeldner M. 2018a. Divide and conquer: the authority of human nature and why we disagree about human nature. E Hannon, T Lewens (eds.), *Why we disagree about human nature* (pp. 186–206). Oxford University Press.

Kronfeldner M. 2018b. *What is left of human nature?* MIT Press.

Kropotkin P. 1902. *Mutual aid*. McClure Phillips.

Labriola A. 1903. *Essays on the materialistic conception of history*. Kerr & Co.

Labriola A. 1907. *Socialism and philosophy*. Kerr & Co.

Labriola A. 1965. *La concezione materialistica della storia*. Laterza.

Labriola A. 2014. *Tutti gli scritti filosofici e di teoria dell'educazione*. Bompiani.

Laland K. 2017. *Darwin's unfinished symphony*. Princeton University Press.

Laland K, Brown G. 2011. *Sense and nonsense*. Oxford University Press.

Laland K, Brown G. 2018. The social construction of human nature. E Hannon, T Lewens (eds.), *Why we disagree about human nature* (pp. 127–44). Oxford University Press.

Laland K, Uller T, Feldman M, Sterelny K, Müller GB, Moczek A, Jablonka E, Odling-Smee J, Wray GA, Hoekstra HE, Futuyma DJ, Lenski RE, Mackay

TFC, Schluter D, Strassmann. 2014. Does evolutionary theory need a rethink? *Nature* 514:7521, pp. 161–4.
Lee RB. 1988. Reflections on primitive communism. T Ingold, D Riches, J Woodburn (eds.), *Hunters and gatherers*, vol. 1 (pp. 252–68). Berg.
Lehrman D. 1970. Semantic & conceptual issues in the nature-nurture problem. D Lehrman (ed.), *Development & evolution of behaviour* (pp. 17–52). Freeman.
Lemetti J. 2011. *Historical dictionary of Hobbes*. Scarecrow Press.
Lennox J. 1993. Darwin was a teleologist. *Biology & Philosophy* 8, pp. 408–21.
Levi P. 2001. *The voice of memory*. Polity.
Levidow L, Pellizzoni L. 2022. Technoscience. B Skeggs, S Farris, A Toscano, S Bromberg (eds.), *The SAGE Handbook of Marxism* (pp. 940–58). SAGE.
Levins R, Lewontin RC. 1985. *The dialectical biologist*. Harvard University Press.
Lewens T. 2009. What is wrong with typological thinking? *Philosophy of Science* 76, pp. 355–71.
Lewens T. 2012a. Human nature: the very idea. *Philosophy & Technology* 25, pp. 459–74.
Lewens T. 2012b. Species, essence and explanation. *Studies in History and Philosophy of Biological and Biomedical Sciences* 43, pp. 751–7.
Lewens T. 2018. Introduction. E Hannon, T Lewens (eds.), *Why we disagree about human nature* (pp. 58–75). Oxford University Press.
Lewis S. 2019. *Full surrogacy now*. Verso.
Lewontin R. 1983. Gene, organism and environment. DS Bendall (ed.), *Evolution from molecules to men* (pp. 271–85). Cambridge University Press.
Lewontin R. 2000. *The triple helix*. Harvard University Press.
Lewontin R, Rose S, Kamin L. 1984. *Not in our genes*. Pantheon.
Lichtman R. 1990. The production of human nature by means of human nature. *Capitalism, Nature, Socialism*, 1:4, pp. 13–51.
Lienemann B. 2021. Aristotle on the rationality of women. P, Adamson, C Rapp (eds.) Adamson P, Rapp C (eds.), *State and nature*. (pp. 135–55). De Gruyter.
Liguori G. 2004. Ideologia. F Frosini, G Liguori (eds.), *Le parole di Gramsci* (pp. 131–49). Carocci.
Liguori G. 2009. Common sense in Gramsci. J Francese (ed.), *Perspectives on Gramsci* (ch. 9). Routledge.
Lloyd E. 2005. *The case against the female orgasm*. Harvard University Press.
Lloyd G. 2013. Aristotle on the natural sociability, skills and intelligence of animals. V Harte, M Lane (eds.), *Politeia in Greek and Roman Philosophy* (pp. 277–93). Cambridge University Press.
Losurdo D. 1997. *Antonio Gramsci: dal liberalismo al "comunismo critico."* Gamberetti.
Losurdo D. 2004. *Hegel and the freedom of moderns*. Duke University Press.
Losurdo D. 2009. *Marx e il bilancio storico del Novecento*. Scuola di Pitagora.

Losurdo D. 2010. Materialismo della prima e materialismo della seconda natura. N Ordine (ed.), *La lezione di un maestro: omaggio a Sebastiano Timpanaro*. Liguori.

Losurdo D. 2011. *Liberalism: a counterhistory*. Verso.

Losurdo D. 2016. *Class struggle: a political and philosophical history*. Palgrave Macmillan.

Losurdo D. 2019. *Nietzsche: the aristocratic rebel*. Brill.

Lussana F. 2006. Gramsci e la Sardegna: socialismo e socialsardismo dagli anni giovanili alla grande Guerra. *Studi Storici* 47:3, pp. 609–35.

Machery E. 2008. A plea for human nature. *Philosophical Psychology* 21, pp. 321–9.

Machery E. 2012. Reconceptualizing human nature: response to Lewens. *Philosophy & Technology* 25, pp. 475–8.

Machery E. 2016. Human nature. DL Smith (ed.), *How biology shapes philosophy* (pp. 204–26). Cambridge University Press.

Machery E. 2018. Doubling down on the nomological notion of human nature. E Hannon, T Lewens (eds.), *Why we disagree about human nature* (pp. 18–39). Oxford University Press.

Machery E. 2021. A new challenge to conceptual engineering. *Inquiry*.

Mackay R, Avanessian A. 2014. *#Accelerate#*. Urbanomic.

Mameli M. 2005. The inheritance of features. *Biology & Philosophy* 20, pp. 365–99.

Mameli M. 2008. On innateness. *Journal of Philosophy* 105:12, pp. 719–36.

Mameli M, Bateson P. 2006. Innateness and the sciences. *Biology & Philosophy* 21, pp. 155–88.

Mameli M, Bateson P. 2011. An evaluation of the concept of innateness. *Philosophical Transactions of the Royal Society B* 366:1563, pp. 436–43.

Mameli M, Del Savio L. 2018. *Darwin, Marx e il mondo globalizzato*. Meltemi.

Markus G. 1978. *Marxism and anthropology*. Van Gorcun.

Marx K. 1974. *The ethnological notebooks* (L Krader, ed.). Van Gorcun.

Marx K, Engels F. 1956–1999. *Werke*. Dietz [MEW].

Marx K, Engels F. 1975–2004. *Collected Works*. Lawrence & Wishart. [MECW].

Matthen M. 2013. Teleology in living things. G Anagnostopolous (ed.), *A Companion to Aristotle*. Wiley-Blackwell.

Maynard-Smith J. 1982. *Evolution and the theory of games*. Cambridge University Press.

Maynard-Smith J. 1998. *Evolutionary genetics*. Oxford University Press.

Maynard-Smith J, Szathmàry E. 1998. *The major transitions in evolution*. Oxford University Press.

Mayr E. 1959. Typological versus population thinking. B Meggers (ed.), *Evolution and anthropology* (pp. 409–12). Anthropological Society of Washington.

McMurtry J. 1978. *The structure of Marx's world view*. Princeton University Press.

McKittrick K. 2015. *Sylvia Wynter: on being human as praxis*. Duke University Press.

Mellars P, Stringer C (eds.). 1989. *The human revolution*. Princeton University Press.

Mészâros I. 1970. *Marx's theory of alienation*. Merlin.

Michalczyk Ł, Dudziak M, Radwan J, Tomkins JL. 2018. Fitness consequences of threshold trait expression subject to environmental cues. *Proceedings of the Royal Society B* 285:20180783.

Mies M, Shiva V. 1993. *Ecofeminism*. Zed.

Moloney P. 2011. Hobbes, savagery, and international anarchy. *The American Political Science Review* 105:1, pp. 189–204.

Mondolfo R. 1912. *Il materialismo storico in Federico Engels*. Formíggini.

Moore J (ed.). 2016. *Anthropocene or capitalocene*? PM Press.

Morgan LH. 1877. *Ancient society*. Holt.

More M, Vita-More N. 2013. *The transhumanist reader*. Wyley.

Morera E. 2014. *Gramsci, materialism, and philosophy*. Routledge.

Morite R, Southwick E. 1992. *Bees as superorganisms*. Springer.

Moron F. 1995. Of pongos and men: Orangs-Outang in Rousseau's Discourse on Inequality. *Review of Politics*, 57:4, pp. 641–64.

Muñoz-Arroyo S, Rodríguez-Jaramillo C, Balart EF. 2019. The goby *Lythrypnus pulchellus* is a bi-directional sex changer. *Environmental Biology of Fishes* 102, pp. 1377–91.

Mustè M. 2021. *Marxism and philosophy of praxis*. Palgrave Macmillan.

Musto M. 2016. *L'ultimo Marx*. Donzelli.

Muthukrishna M, Henrich J, Slingerland E. 2021. Psychology as a historical science. *Annual Review of Psychology* 72, pp. 717–49.

Newman SA. 2022. Marxism and new materialism. *Marxism and Sciences* 1:2, pp. 1–12.

Nussbaum M. 1992. Human functioning and social justice: in defense of Aristotelian essentialism. *Political Theory* 20:2, pp. 202–46.

Nussbaum M. 1995. Aristotle on human nature and the foundations of ethics. J Altan, R Harrison (eds.), *World, mind, and ethics* (pp. 86–131). Cambridge University Press.

Odling-Smee FJ. 1988. Niche-constructing phenotypes. HC Plotkin (ed.), *The role of behavior in evolution* (pp. 73–132). MIT Press.

Odling-Smee FJ, Laland KN, Feldman MW. 2003. *Niche construction*. Princeton University Press.

Okasha S. 2002. Darwinian metaphysics: species and the question of essentialism. *Synthese* 131, pp. 191–213.

Ottaviano C. 1982. Antonio Labriola e il problema dell'espansione coloniale. *Annali della Fondazione Einaudi* XVI, pp. 305–28.
Pagden A. 1982. *The fall of natural man*. Cambridge University Press.
Pearce T. 2014a. The dialectical biologist, circa 1890: John Dewey and the Oxford Hegelians. *Journal of the History of Philosophy* 52:4, pp. 747–77.
Pearce T. 2014b. The origins and development of the idea of organism-environment interaction. G Barker et al. (eds.), *Entangled life* (pp. 13–32). Springer.
Pellicano E, den Houting J. 2022. Shifting from 'normal science' to neurodiversity in autism science. *Journal of Child Psychology and Psychiatry* 63:4, pp. 381–96.
Pestelli C. 2013. *L'universo leopardiano di Sebastiano Timpanaro e altri saggi su Leopardi e sulla famiglia*. Polistampa.
Pettit P. 2008. *Made with words*. Princeton University Press.
Phillips A. 2015. *The politics of the human*. Cambridge University Press.
Phillips A. 2020. Rescuing the human from human nature. *Critical Quarterly* 62:3, pp. 48–52.
Phillips A. 2021. *Unconditional equals*. Princeton University Press.
Pink T. 2016. Hobbes, liberty, action, and free will. HP Martinich, K Hoekstra (eds.), *Oxford Handbook to Hobbes* (pp. 171–94). Oxford University Press.
Pink T. Forthcoming. Introduction to Thomas Hobbes, *Of libertie and necessitie; Questions concerning liberty, necessity, and chance*. Clarendon.
Pinker S. 1994. *The language instinct*. Allen Lane.
Pinker S. 1997. *How the mind works*. Norton.
Pinker S. 2002. *The blank slate*. Viking.
Pinker S. 2011. *The better angels of our nature*. Viking.
Planer R, Sterelny K. 2021. *From signal to symbol*. MIT Press.
Plavcan JM. 2012. Sexual size dimorphism, canine dimorphism, and male-male competition in primates: where do humans fit in? *Human Nature* 23, pp. 47–65.
Prum R. 2017. *The evolution of beauty*. Anchor.
Ramsey G. 2013. Human nature in a post-essentialist world. *Philosophy of Science* 80:5, pp. 983–93.
Ramsey G. 2018. Trait bin and trait clusters accounts of human nature. E Hannon, T Lewens (eds.), *Why we disagree about human nature* (pp. 40–57). Oxford University Press.
Ricardo D. 1817. *On the principles of political economy and taxation*. Murray.
Richards E. 2017. *Darwin and the making of sexual selection*. University of Chicago Press.
Roes F. 1998. An interview of Edward O. Wilson. *Human Ethology Bulletin* 13:1, pp. 6–9.

Rosenthal G, Ryan M. 2022. Sexual selection and the ascent of women: Mate choice research since Darwin. *Science* 375:6578.
Rossi A. 2014. *Gramsci in carcere*. Guida.
Roughgarden J. 2004. *Evolution's rainbow*. University of California Press.
Roughley N. 2021. Human nature. *Stanford Encyclopedia of Philosophy*, https:// plato.stanford.edu.
Rousseau JJ. 1979. *Emile*. Basic Books.
Rousseau JJ. 1990. *Rousseau judge of Jean-Jacques: dialogues*. Dartmouth College Press.
Rousseau JJ. 2007. *Oeuvres complètes: Tome III*. Gallimard.
Rousseau JJ. 2009. *Essay on the origins of languages and writings related to music*. Dartmouth College Press.
Rousseau JJ. 2012. *The major political writings of Jean-Jacques Rousseau* (JT Scott, ed.). University of Chicago Press.
Sahlins M. 2008. *The Western illusion of human nature*. University of Chicago Press.
Saito K. 2023. *Marx in the Anthropocene*. Cambridge University Press.
Samuels R. 2012. Science and human nature. *Royal Institute of Philosophy Supplement* 70, pp. 1–28.
Sandel M. 2008. *The case against perfection*. Harvard University Press.
Savulescu J, Bostrom N (eds.). 2009. *Human enhancement*. Oxford University Press.
Sayers S. 1998. *Marx and human nature*. Routledge.
Schaff P (ed.) 1887. *Nicene and Post-Nicene Fathers*, vol. V. Christian Literature Company.
Schmid K. 2008. Loss of immortality? Hermeneutical aspects of *Genesis* 2–3 and its early receptions. K Schmid, C Riedweg (eds.), *Beyond Eden* (pp. 58–78). Mohr Siebeck.
Sclocco C. 2021. Antonio Gramsci e le scienze sperimentali. *Consecutio Rerum* 10.
Sheehan E. 1993. *Marxism and the philosophy of science*. Humanities Press International.
Sinervo B, Lively BM. 1996. The rock-paper-scissors game and the evolution of alternative male strategies. *Nature*. 380:6571, pp. 240–3.
Singer P. 1999. *A Darwinian left*. Weidenfeld & Nicolson.
Skinner Q. 2009. The material presentation of Thomas Hobbes's theory of the Commonwealth. D Colas, O Kharkhordin (eds.), *The materiality of Res Publica* (pp. 115–58). Cambridge Scholars.
Slotten R. 2004. *The heretic in Darwin's court*. Columbia University Press.
Smith A. 1975. *An inquiry into the nature and causes of the wealth of nations*. Oxford University Press.

Smith DL. 2020. *On inhumanity*. Oxford University Press.
Smith MS. 2019. *The Genesis of good and evil*. Westminster John Knox Press.
Sober E. 1980. Evolution, population thinking, and essentialism. *Philosophy of Science* 47, pp. 350–83.
Sober E, Wilson DS. 1997. *Unto others*. Harvard University Press.
Solinas M. 2015. *From Aristotle's teleology to Darwin's genealogy*. Palgrave Macmillan.
Sorell T. 1999. Hobbes and Aristotle. C Blackwell, S Kurukawa (eds.), *Philosophy in the sixteenth and seventeenth centuries: conversations with Aristotle*. Routledge.
Sparrow R. 2015. Imposing genetic diversity. *American Journal of Bioethics* 15:6, pp. 2–10.
Spelke EK, Breilinger J, Macomber J, Jacobsen K. 1992. Origins of knowledge. *Psychological Review* 99, pp. 605–32.
Stack D. 2003. *The first Darwinian left*. New Clarion.
Sterelny K. 2012. *The evolved apprentice*. MIT Press.
Sterelny K. 2018. Sceptical reflections on human nature. E Hannon, T Lewens (eds.), *Why we disagree about human nature* (pp. 107–26). Oxford University Press.
Sterelny K. 2021. *The Pleistocene social contract*. Oxford University Press.
Sterelny K, Griffiths PE. 1999. *Sex and death*. University of Chicago Press.
Stotz K, Griffiths PE. 2018. A developmental systems account of human nature. E Hannon, T Lewens (ed.) *Why we disagree about human nature* (pp. 58–75). Oxford University Press.
Struhl KJ. 2016. Marx and human nature: the historical, the trans-historical, and human flourishing. *Science & Society* 80:1, pp. 78–104.
Stuurman S. 2017. *Inventing humanity*. Harvard University Press.
Thomas P. 2021. *Marxism and scientific socialism*. Routledge.
Thomas PD. 2009. *The Gramscian moment*. Brill.
Thomasson A. 2021. Conceptual engineering: when do we need it? How can we do it? *Inquiry*.
Timpanaro S. 1970. *Sul materialismo*. Nistri-Lischi.
Timpanaro S. 1975. *On materialism*. NLB.
Timpanaro S. 1976. *The Freudian slip*. NLB.
Timpanaro S. 1982. *Antileopardiani e neomoderati nella sinistra italiana*. ETS.
Timpanaro S. 1995. *Nuovi studi sul nostro Ottocento*. Nistri-Lischi.
Timpanaro S. 2001. *Il verde e il rosso* (L Cortesi, ed.). Odradek.
Timpanaro S. 2011. *Classicismo e illuminismo nell'Ottocento italiano* (C Pestelli, ed.). Le Lettere.
Toivanen J. 2021. *The political animal in medieval philosophy*. Brill.

Tomasello M 2019. *Becoming human*. Harvard University Press.
Trivers R. 2002. *Natural selection and social theory*. Oxford University Press.
Vegetti M, Ademollo F. 2016. *Incontro con Aristotele*. Einaudi.
Von Rohr CR, Coski SE, Burkart JM, Caws C, Orlaith NF, Ziltener A, van Shaik CP. 2012. Impartial third-party interventions in captive chimpanzees: a reflection of community concern. *PloS One* 7:3, p. e32494.
Waddington CH. 1968. Towards a theoretical biology. *Nature* 218, pp. 525–7.
Wallace AR. 1864. The origin of human races and the antiquity of man deduced from the theory of natural selection. *Journal of the Anthropological Society of London* 2, pp. clviii–clxxxvi.
Wallace AR. 1870. *Contributions to the theory of natural selection*. Macmillan.
Wallace AR. 1890. Human selection. *Fortnightly Review* 48, p. 137.
Wallace AR. 1892. Human progress: past and future. *Arena* 5, pp. 145–59.
Wallace AR. 1913. *Social environment and moral progress*. Cassell.
Walsh D. 2006. Evolutionary essentialism. *British Journal for the Philosophy of Science* 57, pp. 425–48.
Walsh D. 2021. Aristotle and contemporary biology. *Cambridge companion to Aristotle's biology* (pp. 280–97). Cambridge University Press.
West-Eberhard MJ. 2003. *Developmental plasticity and evolution*. Oxford University Press.
Whitfield J. 2002. The police state. *Nature* 416, pp. 782–4.
Wiley AS. 2018. Lactase persistence. W Trevathan (ed.) *The international encyclopedia of biological anthropology*. Wyley.
Williams R. 1980. *Problems in culture and materialism*. Verso.
Wilson B. 2007. *The hive*. St. Martin's.
Wilson EO. 1971. *The insect societies*. Harvard University Press.
Wilson EO. 1975. *Sociobiology*. Harvard University Press.
Wilson EO. 1978. *Human nature*. Harvard University Press.
Wilson R. 1999. Realism, essence, and kind: resuscitating species essentialism? R Wilson (ed.) *Species* (pp. 187–208). MIT Press.
Wokler R. 1978. Perfectible apes in decadent cultures: Rousseau's anthropology revisited. *Daedalus* 107:3, pp. 107–34.
Wokler R. 2001. *Rousseau*. Oxford University Press.
Woodburn J. 1982. Egalitarian societies. *Man* 17, pp. 431–51.
Wrangham R. 2009. *Catching fire*. Basic Books.
Wrangham R. 2019. *The goodness paradox*. Penguin Random House.
Wynter S. 1995. 1492: A new world view. E Wynter, VH Lawrence, R Nettleford (eds.), *Race, discourse, and the origin of the Americas* (pp. 5–57). Smithsonian Institution Press.

Wynter S. 2001. Towards the sociogenic principle: Fanon, identity, the puzzle of conscious experience, and what it is like to be "Black." MF Durán-Cogan, A Gómez-Moriana (eds.), *National identities and socio-political changes in Latin America* (pp. 30–66). Routledge.

Wynter S. 2003. Unsettling the coloniality of being/power/truth/freedom: towards the human, after Man, its overrepresentation—an argument. *The New Centennial Review* 3:3, pp. 257–337.

Zuk M, Simmon LW. 2018. *Sexual selection*. Oxford University Press.

Index